SHAKESPEARE COUNTRY

GREAT LITTLE GUIDES

Compact Guide: Shakespeare Country is the ideal quick-reference guide to the landscape that inspired England's greatest poet and playwright. It covers all the region's attractions: the famous sites of Stratford-upon-Avon, the mighty castles of Warwick and Kenilworth, fine country houses and world-famous gardens, the quaint villages of the Cotswolds, and the modern cities of Coventry and Birmingham.

This is one of almost 100 titles in *Apa Publications'* acclaimed series of pocket-sized, easy-to-use guide-books intended for the independent-minded traveller. *Compact Guides* are in essence travel encyclopedias in miniature, designed to be comprehensive yet portable, as well as up-to-date and authoritative.

Star Attractions

An instant reference to some of Shakespeare Country's top attractions to help you set your priorities.

Shakespeare's Birthplace p15

Hall's Croft p21

Royal Shakespeare Theatre p22

Anne Hathaway's Cottage p23

Lord Leycester's Hospital, Warwick p25

Kenilworth Castle p32

Mary Arden's House p34

Packwood House p35

Hidcote Manor Garden p47

Warwick Castle p28

Coventry Cathedral p57

SHAKESPEARE COUNTRY

Introduction

Shakespeare Country – Mid-most England......................................5
Historical Highlights...10

Places

Route 1: Stratford-upon-Avon...**14**
Route 2: Warwick, Leamington and Kenilworth..........................**24**
Route 3: Into Arden **34**
Route 4: Westwards towards Bromsgrove...................................**38**
Route 5: Southeast from Stratford...**42**
Route 6: In and out of the Cotswolds...**47**
Route 7: Birmingham **52**
Route 8: Coventry..**56**

Culture

Stratford and the Cult of Shakespeare **61**
Warwickshire in the History of the Nation **63**
The Buildings of Shakespeare Country **64**
Festivals, Events and Entertainment..**65**

Leisure

Food and Drink **67**
Active Pursuits **70**

Practical Information

Getting There **73**
Getting Around **74**
Facts for the Visitor..**75**
Shakespeare Country for Children..**76**
Accommodation...**77**

Index **80**

Shakespeare Country – Mid-most England

'Mid-most England, unmitigated England…' was the novelist Henry James's attempt to sum up the character of his much-loved Warwickshire. In many ways, the Shakespeare country of the Avon and its tributaries does seem to encapsulate those quintessential English qualities sought by natives and visitors alike. Here, never far from the banks of a slow-flowing river, is that utterly English patchwork quilt of small hedged fields, a deep green setting for the occasional country town and villages of timber-framed or mellow brick houses. There are great castles, fine manor houses, and a wealth of parklands and gardens, all linked by a dense network of country roads and lanes.

Feeding the swans in Stratford

Though undoubtedly much has changed since Shakespeare's time, this intricately textured landscape seems to hold not only the memory of the playwright himself but of the rural scenes which inspired so much of the rich imagery of his writing. What has changed since his time is the ring of towns to the north. But even 400 years ago, places like Coventry and Birmingham were already distinct centres of commerce and manufacturing whose greatest days were to come in the 19th and 20th centuries. Today they offer the visitor all the cultural and recreational attractions of great cities, an intriguing and invigorating contrast to the rural delights of southern Warwickshire and Worcestershire's Vale of Evesham.

5

Landscapes and townscapes

The scenery of Shakespeare country is tranquil rather than spectacular. The landscape consists of well-watered vales between which undulating country never rises higher than 500ft (150m). The most distinct feature, visible from much of the southern part of the area, is the Cotswold escarpment which reaches a height of 854ft (260m) above the village of Ilmington and more than 1,000ft (300m) above Broadway. Continuing in an easterly direction is a less dramatic escarpment, though Edge Hill, scene of a famous Civil War battle, is a commanding presence.

Historic Warwick

From its source near Naseby in Northamptonshire, the Avon flows for nearly 100 miles (160km) before joining the Severn at Tewkesbury. Its meandering course is generally accompanied by lush green meadows, but at Guy's Cliff, just upstream from Warwick, it is overlooked by a rocky bluff, then by another at Warwick itself. This forms a magnificent site for what is justifiably described as one of England's most magnificent strongholds, whose walls and towers loom high above the river and the luxuriant parkland laid out on its banks. The castle shields the Avon from the town that

Kenilworth Castle ruin

grew up under its protection, and which is a wonderful amalgam of all the building styles and materials that occur in the region, from late medieval black and white timber-framed houses to variations of the theme of Georgian brick, stone and stucco. Much more homogenous is neighbouring Leamington Spa, whose dignified terraces, crescents and public buildings were built for the leisured classes of 19th-century Britain who came here to seek health from the waters and entertainment from each other.

Another near neighbour is Kenilworth Castle, equal in magnificence and atmosphere to Warwick despite its ruined state. Between them the two castles tell much of the history of England in stone, from the days of the Normans to the great magnates of the late Middle Ages like 'Kingmaker' Richard Neville, and from the to-ings and fro-ings of opposing armies in the Civil War to relatively modern times, when Warwick was one of the social centres of the Edwardian elite. And history is indeed made to come alive in both places, among the evocative ruins of Kenilworth by courtesy of English Heritage and its pageants, and at Warwick thanks to the ingenuity of its newest owners, Madame Tussaud's, who have peopled the interior with convincing reconstructions of castle life.

Parks and gardens

The parklands of Warwick Castle announce one of the other themes of Shakespeare Country. Here is a landscape exceptionally rich not only in country houses of all periods but in the parks and gardens which ornament them.

Despite its location on the very fringe of the Birmingham conurbation, the setting of Baddesley Clinton Hall is particularly idyllic, while the moated hall itself has been called 'the perfect late medieval manor house'. Nearby Packwood House has formal gardens which perfectly rep-

Baddesley Clinton Hall

Warwick Castle

resent the feeling of Tudor times, even though the famous Yew Garden has been shown to be of relatively recent origin. Compton Wynyates, one of Warwickshire's – indeed England's – most picturesque country houses, also boasted a topiary garden of great charm, though this has recently been destroyed and the house is no longer open to the public.

Capability Brown and his 18th-century contemporaries re-landscaped much of the Shakespearean scene, not only at Warwick Castle, but at Charlecote Park, where the Avon is joined by one of its pretty tributaries, the Dene. Here, Brown was made to spare the formal avenues of the parkland which encompasses the meeting of the rivers and which, traditionally, was the scene of the young Shakespeare's deer-poaching activities. The formal, Dutch-style gardens of Hanbury Hall near Bromsgrove were swept away in Brown's time but are now being conscientiously restored. The lavish borders and secret enclosures of one of the great trend-setting gardens of the early 20th century, Hidcote Manor, can be admired on top of the Cotswold scarp near Chipping Campden, together with an equally appealing modern garden, Kiftsgate Court.

Hidcote Manor gardens

Arden and Feldon

The hill country of the Cotswolds and their extension eastwards overlooks that part of the Warwickshire lowland traditionally known as the Feldon, quite distinct from the Arden on the far bank of the Avon. The clay soils and flatter countryside of the Feldon were cleared for farming far earlier than the densely forested Arden country, where woodland persisted until relatively recently.

The Feldon always had a more open appearance, with larger fields and fewer hedgerow trees, while the undulating Arden, which was only slowly and laboriously taken into cultivable land, has a much more irregular pattern of small fields, scattered hamlets and farmsteads and, even today, far more woodland. Its charm worked its spell on Shakespeare, who made it the Arcadian setting for the frolics of *A Midsummer Night's Dream*. The distinction between these two types of countryside is beautifully brought out in the wonderful 16th-century Sheldon tapestry map of Warwickshire displayed in Warwick Museum.

In the 1970s the landscapes of Shakespeare Country, like the rest of southern Britain, were subjected to the ravages of Dutch elm disease. In Warwickshire and the Vale of Evesham the effects were particularly disastrous. The elm had been known as the 'Warwickshire weed', in places making up half the total of hedgerow trees and contributing in no small measure to the epithet of 'leafy Warwicks'. Today it is difficult to imagine the landscape as it was, with elms forming an almost continuous, dense green screen

Traditional Arden thatch,
Shakespeare Countryside Museum

along the hedgerows in many places, inhibiting long views but contributing to a feeling of intimacy and cosiness which nowadays is perhaps experienced more in the villages than in the newly opened-up countryside.

Benefiting from its position between the Arden and the Feldon is Stratford-upon-Avon. Glorying in the name of Shakespeare, the town is far more than a shrine to his memory, though it certainly is that, with an array of 'Shakespearean' attractions as well as the houses in the guardianship of the Birthplace Trust and the Royal Shakespeare Theatre with its triple auditoriums.

While Warwick lives in the shadow of its castle, and Leamington is essentially a residential town, Stratford is the market centre for a broad tract of south Warwickshire, a focal point of highways, though no longer of railways. It's a pleasure to be here, among ancient buildings or on the sleek river bank, even without a thought of Shakespeare in one's head. But it would be wrong to expect to be on one's own; Stratford is England's most popular tourist town outside London.

Bustling Stratford

Vales and hills

Downstream from Stratford, the Avon winds westward into the Vale of Evesham, whose varied, mostly well-drained soils and relatively dry climate have long made it one of England's great market garden regions, famed in monastic times for its cider and perry (pear cider). The trees here are orchard species or poplars grown as windbreaks, sheltering the valuable crops of fruit and vegetables grown in the countless small and intensively worked plots. The local asparagus is famous, served as a seasonal speciality in pubs and restaurants along the Avon, which bends accommodatingly to make a well-protected site for the old abbey town of Evesham, site of a great battle in 1265 in which Simon de Montfort's baronial challenge to the king was crushed.

Vale of Evesham from the Cotswolds

Beyond the great mound of Bredon Hill and several giant meanders downstream is pretty Pershore, the Georgian character of its streets beautifully preserved. Bredon is an outlier of the Cotswolds, whose outline several miles away forms a more or less continuous backdrop to this trip down the Avon. No visitor should miss the opportunity to see at least something of this enchanting area, some of whose finest small towns and villages like Chipping Campden and Broadway are within easy reach.

Chipping Campden

Midland cities

This seemingly changeless countryside along the Avon is linked by road, rail and canal to the northern part of Warwickshire, where urban influences gradually, or in some places abruptly, become apparent. Kenilworth is separated

from Coventry only by a narrow green belt containing the modern University of Warwick and the city's airport. Coventry now has its own university, the former Lanchester Polytechnic, academic focus of the city's great craft and engineering tradition which made it one of the centres of Britain's motor industry. The town's modern fame stems from the disaster which overtook it in 1940, when a German air raid destroyed its centre and its cathedral. The subsequent rebuilding of both established Coventry as a symbol of hope and progress in the postwar era.

To the west of Coventry, in the green belt which keeps the city distinct from Birmingham, is the village of Meriden, the place whose strong claim to be the geographical centre of England is marked by the stone cross on its green. This is motorway country, close to the meeting point of the M6 and M42 and other major roads, an ideally central location not only for Birmingham airport, one of Britain's busiest, but also for the huge halls of the National Exhibition Centre which attracts 4 million visitors annually, many of them arriving via its own rail station.

It is here, as much as in Birmingham city centre, that one feels the dynamism of the vast urban region of the West Midlands which extends beyond Birmingham itself into the conurbation of the Black Country. Birmingham had become an industrial centre long before the Industrial Revolution of the late 18th century. The canals and railways of that era confirmed its importance, while in more recent times it has become the focus of the national motorway network. Like other dynamic cities with a once powerful manufacturing base, Birmingham is reinventing itself as a great centre for services, shopping and cultural activities, claiming for itself not merely a national but also a European role as it looks to the future. The city is just half an hour away from Shakespeare Country, but the contrast couldn't be greater.

Long tradition in Coventry: Lady Godiva

Coventry Cathedral rebuilt

Along Birmingham's canals

Prehistory

As the climate warmed up at the end of the last Ice Age some 10,000 years ago, the ice sheets covering the Midlands retreated northwards leaving behind a tundra-like landscape which was gradually colonised by trees. First birch, then alder and willow spread across what is now Warwickshire, followed by lime, oak and elm, with, eventually, some beech on the higher, better-drained ground of the hill country to the south of the Avon. Often characterised as wild and impenetrable, this midland forest certainly seems to have inhibited human settlement, though in recent years much evidence has come to light of human activity, particularly on the gravel terraces along the courses of the present rivers.

The area has no great prehistoric monuments to compare with the henges and other features of the chalk downlands of Wessex, though on the higher ground to the south of the Avon stand several Bronze or Iron Age earthworks such as Nadbury Camp on Edge Hill or the fort on the isolated summit of Meon Hill. The Red Horse which once ornamented the slopes of Edge Hill and was the equal of the more famous White Horse of Uffington has long since been obliterated.

Roman times

The Romans too seem to have accepted the natural constraints of these damp, well-wooded lowlands, though their strategic highways penetrate the area. Linking Lincoln to Cirencester and Bath, the great road now known as the Foss Way also marked the outer limit of the province established in southeast England. Today part A-road, part B-road, it still serves as a cross-country route of some importance, avoiding the main towns like Stratford, Warwick, Leamington and Coventry.

The other main Roman road in the area, Ryknild Street, left the Foss Way near Stow-on-the-Wold and ran north via Alcester, the only Roman settlement of any size in the area, crossing the Birmingham plateau to join Watling Street. A minor road from the Roman salt workings at Droitwich cut through the dense Forest of Feckenham to the east, then crossed the Avon by a ford where the town of Stratford now stands.

The Anglo-Saxon settlement

After the breakdown of Roman rule the area was colonised by groups of settlers making their way inland along the river valleys. The Saxon Hwicce followed the course of the Severn and Avon, avoiding the heavy clay soils of the thickly wooded Arden and establishing themselves on the river gravels, particularly around Bidford-on-Avon and Stratford. For a while the Arden seems to have acted as a buffer zone separating them from the Anglian tribes to the north who later came together to form the kingdom of Mercia.

At the Battle of Cirencester in AD628 the Mercian King Penda defeated the Hwicce and brought their lands into his realm, though their own leaders continued to rule under his authority. Penda was a pagan, but his son Peada was a Christian and much of present-day Warwickshire became part of the bishopric he established at Lichfield in the middle of the 7th century. The earliest convents were founded in Coventry (around 650) and at Stratford (around 693). Mercian power continued to grow under powerful King Offa, but after his death the kingdom disintegrated and was unable to resist the onslaught of Egbert, the king of Wessex, who made himself their ruler in 829.

Saxons and Danes

Over the century following their first landing in 787, the Danes managed to conquer most of England north of the Thames. Their power was successfully challenged by the great King Alfred of Wessex and his successors. For a while, the old Roman road of Watling Street formed the boundary of the Danelaw, across which the Danes continued to make destructive incursions. In 889, Alfred's eldest daughter Ethelfleda married Ethelred, a Mercian Earl; after his death in 910 she maintained his rule, building a line of strategic fortresses against the Danes, among which was the great mound at Warwick.

But in 1016 the Danish King Cnut (Canute) organised an irresistible invasion force which crushed all opposition and made the whole country part of the Danish empire until the recall from Normandy of Edward the Confessor. One of Canute's chief lieutenants was Leofric, who, together with his wife Godiva founded the great Benedictine abbey of Coventry in 1043.

Despite destructive wars and wholesale depredations, by the 11th century the rural settlement pattern was virtually complete, the close-spaced network of villages and hamlets much the same as it is today.

1066 The Saxon lord of Warwick, Earl Turchil, takes no part in King Harold's resistance to William of Normandy, and is allowed by the Conqueror to keep his castle and all his lands, though at his death they go to Henry de Newburgh, who becomes the first Norman Earl of Warwick.

c1120 A Norman motte and bailey castle constructed at Kenilworth. Other castles of this type erected at Brailes, Kineton, and Beaudesert at Henley-in-Arden.

1262 Under Simon de Montfort, Kenilworth Castle is the focal point of the Barons' insurrection against King Henry III. The King and Prince Edward are imprisoned in the castle in 1264, but the rising is brought to an end at the Battle of Evesham in 1265 at which de Montfort is killed.

1348 Bubonic plague, known as the Black Death, ravages the country, killing up to half the population, and resulting in the abandonment of many villages. The profitability of sheep farming encourages landowners to drive peasant tenants from their land in favour of great sheep ranches. By the mid-15th century more than 100 villages in south Warwickshire have disappeared.

c1400 After York, Bristol and London, Coventry is the fourth largest city in England, with a population of around 7,000.

1449 Richard Neville acquires the earldom of Warwick by marriage to Anne Beauchamp. Subsequently known as 'The Kingmaker', he plays a highly manipulative but ultimately unsuccessful role in the Wars of the Roses (*see page 63*).

1535 Dissolution of the monasteries. Their buildings become quarries, raided by local people for building stone and other materials, though Pershore's abbey church is acquired by the townspeople as their parish church.

1564 William, the third child of John and Mary Shakespeare, born at Stratford-upon-Avon.

1575 The fourth visit of Queen Elizabeth I to Kenilworth Castle, held by her favourite Robert Dudley, is the occasion of lavish celebrations. The region shares in the country's general prosperity under the Tudors, and there is much building and rebuilding in both town and country.

1605 Coughton Court is a centre of the Gunpowder Plot conspiracy to blow up the Houses of Parliament.

1642–8 The Civil War. The area is a stronghold of Parliamentary sympathies. Birmingham turns out thousands of swords for the Parliamentary forces and Coventry shuts its gates against King Charles I. The Battle of Edge Hill in 1642 ends indecisively. In 1643, Birmingham is subjected to a vengeful sacking by Prince Rupert, and at the Restoration Coventry is made to demolish its walls.

c1700 Birmingham's rapidly expanding population, including metal-workers, gun-smiths, and button-makers, reaches a total of about 7,000. Later in the 18th century, canal-building confirms the town's commercial and industrial importance, which is reinforced by the arrival, via Coventry, of Britain's first trunk railway, the London and Birmingham, in 1838.

1769 The Shakespearean actor David Garrick organises Jubilee celebrations at Stratford.

1786 The first medicinal baths opened at Leamington Spa.

1879 Stratford's Shakespeare Memorial Theatre completed.

1911 Creation of Greater Birmingham, the second largest city in Britain, with an impressive record of municipal administration and civic improvement.

1932 In Stratford, a new Shakespeare Memorial Theatre replaces the original building, destroyed by fire in 1926.

1940 Now an important centre of vehicle manufacture and armaments production, Coventry suffers severe destruction in the course of a German air raid. The remains of the city's St Michael's Cathedral are incorporated into the new Cathedral of 1962, while the postwar reconstruction of the city centre gains international fame as an example of modern city planning.

1996 Stratford-upon-Avon celebrates the 800th anniversary of the granting of its charter by King Richard I.

The nine-arched bridge over
the Avon

Harvard House

Entering the canal basin

Preceding pages:
Anne Hathaway's Cottage

Route 1

Stratford-upon-Avon

See map on page 16

Stratford-upon-Avon basks in Shakespeare's fame, and Shakespeare is the reason why visitors come here from all over the world: to see the sites associated with the town's most illustrious son, absorb the atmosphere of the streets he once walked, and perhaps attend a performance of one of his plays at the Royal Shakespeare Theatre. Local people come here to work, shop and do business, since Stratford has its own life to lead, as a market town of some importance in this part of the south Midlands. Still others pour into the place to enjoy its charming townscape, to laze away summer hours by the riverside, or to 'mess about in boats', since the town not only has one of the most attractive stretches of the Avon but is also the meeting point of the Stratford Canal with the river.

The town's name, 'street-ford', indicates that this was the point at which a Roman road linking the Foss Way with Ryknild Street crossed the Avon, but Stratford's real origin goes back only to Saxon times, when a monastery flourished here, probably where the parish church now stands, at some distance from the modern town centre. By the end of the 12th century, the little settlement around the church was inadequate to handle the growing agricultural prosperity of the region, and in 1196, the bishop began to build an entirely new town on well-drained land just above the Avon's flood-plain. His slightly-skewed chequerboard layout of the market town still determines Stratford's street pattern today, despite the inevitable re-building that has taken place over the centuries.

Most explorations of Stratford begin at the point where the two bridges over the Avon funnel pedestrian and vehicular traffic into the town, where there is a large car park, the modern Moat House Hotel, and the ever-busy Tourist Information Centre. On the far side of the swirling traffic from these architecturally incongruous additions to the town's amenities is an attractive area of riverside open space, **Bancroft Gardens**. Here, overlooking the narrowboats at their moorings in the canal basin is the first and perhaps the most endearing of all the many images of William Shakespeare to be seen around the town; the **Gower Memorial** of 1888 has the alert figure of the playwright seated alert atop a plinth, surrounded by statues of Hamlet, Prince Hal, Falstaff and Lady Macbeth, representing Philosophy, History, Comedy and Tragedy. Originally the group stood close to the Memorial Theatre, but was moved here in 1933 to ornament the newly laid out gardens and dignify the approach to the town.

Gower Memorial

The pathway from the Gower Memorial leads to the nine-arched brick bridge over the Avon. Built in 1823 for the tramway whose horse-drawn carriages and goods wagons once rattled their way between Stratford and Shipston-on-Stour, it was converted to pedestrian use after the rails were lifted in 1918. It's a good place from which to get a grandstand prospect of the activity on the river with the Memorial Theatre as a backdrop. In addition, there's a side view of the principal river crossing, the **Clopton Bridge**. Completed towards the end of the 15th century, the stone structure was paid for by Sir Hugh Clopton, the Stratford man who became Lord Mayor of London and who 'having never wife nor children convertid a greate peace of his substance in good works in Stratford'. With a little judicious widening in the 19th century, its 14 arches have carried the ever-increasing weight of traffic for more than 500 years.

15

Clopton Bridge

From the bridgefoot, broad Bridge Street rises gently to its junction with the High Street. Its width was sufficient to accommodate a row of houses down the middle, but these have long since been demolished, and the busy scene is now dominated by chain stores which have been fitted into the old buildings with a greater or lesser degree of taste. Partly pedestrianised, Henley Street funnels the crowds towards the complex of buildings around Stratford's outstanding place of pilgrimage, ★★★ **Shakespeare's Birthplace** ❷ (late March to late October Monday to Friday 9am–5pm, Sunday 9.30am–5pm, winter Monday to Saturday 9.30am–4pm, Sunday 10am–4pm). Originally from the nearby village of Snitterfield, William's father, John Shakespeare, set up in Stratford as a glover, wool merchant and money-lender. He was

Shakespeare's Birthplace

Shakespeare's Study

evidently prosperous enough to pay a fine of 12 pence levied on him for allowing rubbish to accumulate in the street in front of his house. Eventually he became important enough to be chosen in 1568 as the town's mayor. The dwelling known as the Birthplace served both as family home and business premises. It's a timber-framed structure dating from the early 16th century, built on a base of stone from the quarries at Wilmcote. In the ownership of Shakespeare descendants until 1806, it was bought in 1847 for the then huge sum of £3,000 by the predecessors of today's Birthplace Trust, the body which administers all five of Stratford's so-called Shakespeare Houses. By that date the building had lost much of its original character, having served as a pub and later as a butcher's shop.

The restoration which began in 1857 has been hailed as exemplary for its time, great care being taken to preserve authenticity and not to reconstruct the building in an over-imaginative way. The Birthplace stands in isolation on the east side of Henley Street, its neighbouring buildings having been pulled down to guard against the risk of fire which had been such a terrible scourge in this largely timber-built town. Its new neighbours include the **Shakespeare Centre**, opened in 1964 to serve as headquarters for the Trust and to house extensive archives, library and study facilities. It is very much a building of its decade, as is the 1981 **Visitors' Centre**. Here is an excellent exhibition entitled

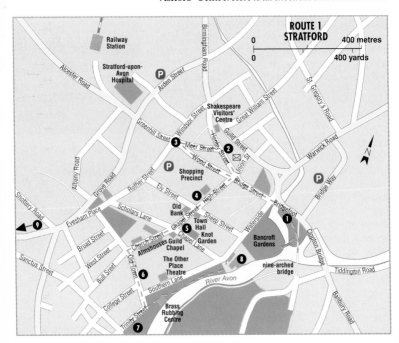

The ubiquitous Bard

'William Shakespeare – His Life and Background' which gives a concise and visually appealing account of the context of the playwright's life in Stratford, London, and finally Stratford again. There are displays on the town of Stratford itself and on the countryside which inspired so much of Shakespeare's imagery. His early life is illustrated, then an array of exhibits evokes his long and successful sojurn in London before his retirement to his native town. There are portraits, furniture, a wonderful model of the Globe Theatre, original documents as well as copies of such items as his marriage licence bond, and an atmospheric reconstruction of 'Shakespeare's Study', the kind of room he may well have worked in. Beyond the Visitors' Centre, the pretty garden has been planted with many of the trees, shrubs and flowers mentioned in the plays.

Shakespeare's Birthplace: the garden

In the Birthplace itself, the rooms which are furnished as far as possible in late 16th-century style as well as having further small-scale displays on aspects of family history and William's work. An upstairs room is, by long tradition, the place where he was born. As in some of the other Trust buildings, the wattle and daub infilling between the structural timbers has been partly exposed. Between 1793 and 1820, the Birthplace was run by Mrs Hornby, an unscrupulous character who, for a small consideration, allowed early literary pilgrims to carve chunks of wood off 'Shakespeare's chair'. Other visitors, including Walter Scott, Henry Irving and Ellen Terry, seem to have been unable to resist the temptation of scratching their names in the glass of the latticed windows, a procedure now definitely frowned on.

Meer Street leads to Rother Street and its centrepiece, the **American Fountain** , an exuberantly ornate clock tower and fountain given to Stratford on the occasion of Queen Victoria's 1887 Jubilee by the Philadelphia news-

American Fountain

paperman, George C. Childs. The site of the cattle market, broad Rother Street is further distinguished by the **White Swan Hotel**, a fine half-timbered building dating originally from the mid-15th century though much restored in the 1920s when highly unusual 16th-century wall paintings were discovered. Other fascinating and equally venerable buildings nearby include No 11 Rother Street and Mason's Court, an example of a Wealden type of house with what was once a central hall open to the roof. Leading back towards Bridge Street and with a number of 16th- and 17th-century buildings, Wood Street once formed one side of a large triangular space bounded by Meer Street and Henley Street which has long since been built over.

Stratford's High Street, together with its continuation along Chapel Street and Church Street, has some of the town's finest buildings, stately timber-framed structures giving way southwards to brick edifices of the Georgian era. The most imposing group of Tudor buildings, all of three storeys and all dating from the end of the 16th century, overlooks the little paved open space at the first crossroads. ★★ **Harvard House** ❹ (late May to late September daily 10am–4pm) has the kind of ornate carving less typical of Warwickshire than of the Welsh Border country, with elaborate bargeboards, friezes, as well as a bull's head, a human face and a particularly fine upright hound. It was built or almost entirely rebuilt following the great fire of 1594 for Thomas Rogers and his wife Alice; their initials, together with the date 1596, can be seen amongst the other carving. Their daughter Katherine married a Robert Harvard and bore him a son, John, who emigrated to America and became the principal benefactor of the university named after him.

The house had many owners and occupants but alone among the High Street's timber buildings was never given a brick or stucco front. After suffering from subsidence, it came to the attention of the popular novelist Marie Corelli, a resident and determined preservationist. In 1909 she persuaded the Chicago millionaire Edward Morris to buy the building, pay for its restoration, and present it to Harvard University. The fascinating interior has 17th-century furniture, displays on John Harvard, and houses part of the extensive Neish Collection of pewter, with pieces ranging from Roman times to the 19th century.

Marie Corelli was also involved in the restoration of the adjoining ★ **Garrick Inn**, some of whose highly decorative timbering dates from a 1912 restoration when the brick facade to which it had been subjected was finally removed. Originally called the Reindeer, it was renamed the Garrick after the 1769 Jubilee organised by the great Shakespearean actor David Garrick (*see page 61*). The

Harvard House hound

The Garrick Inn

8

1963 brick and concrete building opposite which replaced the old Corn Exchange was hailed at the time as a model solution to the problem of fitting new structures into an historic town, but everyone will make their own mind up about how well its fanciful gables and projections have stood the test of time.

The paved area in front of this building makes a good vantage point from which to look briefly at the **Town Hall**. Originally named Shakespeare Hall, this is the 18th-century successor to an earlier building destroyed in the Civil War when a gunpowder store exploded, apparently in an attempt to inconvenience the Parliamentary forces occupying the town. A classical structure in stone, it has an ornamental niche with a statue of Shakespeare which was presented by Garrick. No contrast could be greater than between this sober classical structure in stone and the jolly Victorian red-brick **Old Bank** opposite. But both buildings pay tribute to the Bard, the Town Hall with a statue in an ornamental niche above the north door and the Bank with a mosaic portrait and terracotta panels with scenes from the plays.

Shakespeare at the Old Bank and at the Town Hall

19

Chapel Street continues the timber-framed theme, first with the magnificent many-bayed and gabled **Shakespeare Hotel**, all of 120ft (36m) long. The part nearest the Town Hall seems to have suffered when the Town Hall was blown up; it was given a new facade in brick, which was eventually removed and the timbers reinstated. The contrast between this newer timber studding and the older, time-worn work beyond is quite striking. The corner of Chapel Street and Scholars Lane is dominated by the **Falcon Hotel**; its lower two storeys date from around 1500. Opposite is another property of the Birthplace Trust, ★★ **Nash's House and the Site of New Place ❺** (late

Falcon Hotel

Nash's House

March to late October Monday to Saturday 9.30am– 5pm, Sunday 10am–5pm, winter Monday to Saturday 10am–4pm, Sunday 10.30am–4pm). Nash's House was bought by the Trust in 1862 and restored early in the 20th century, not only because of its intrinsic interest – it was the home of Shakespeare's grand-daughter, Elizabeth Hall – but because its garden was laid out over the remains of New Place, the dwelling Shakespeare bought in 1597 as a retreat from London and retirement home. Elizabeth became the wife of the lawyer Thomas Nash after whom the house is named in 1626, and survived his death to marry John Barnard, a Northamptonshire landowner.

The three-storey house with its twin gables and overhangs has fine examples of 17th-century furnishings as well as tapestries, portraits and ceramics, and a group of 15th-century carved oak angels from the nearby Guild Chapel. It also houses a museum with archaeological exhibits from the Stratford area and a display on Garrick.

New Place had been constructed by Hugh Clopton around 1480, and when bought by Shakespeare for the sum of £60 was among the finest houses in Stratford; in 1643, it was a fit place for Queen Henrietta Maria to stay as a guest of Elizabeth. It was modernised at the beginning of the 18th century by being given a grand, classical style front in brick, and was then bought by the Reverend Francis Gastrell of Cheshire, who used it as a summer home. An irascible character, Gastrell became so annoyed by visitors pestering him to see the mulberry tree Shakespeare was supposed to have planted in the garden that he had it cut down. Then, after a quarrel with the borough about payment of local taxes, Gastrel, vowing that his house should never again be assessed by impertinent officials, ordered its demolition. All that remains today are two wells and some foundations. Beyond is a **knot garden**, created

Visitors to the site of New Place and the knot garden

after World War I in Tudor style, and further still the **Great Garden**, open to the public, and with two mulberry trees, one supposedly grown from a cutting of the original tree, the other, itself a cutting, planted by the actress Peggy Ashcroft in 1969.

Opposite the site of New Place stands the ★ **Guild Chapel**, a decorous and substantial building which, not surprisingly, is often mistaken for the parish church. Mostly dating from a 15th-century rebuilding financed by Hugh Clopton, it was originally founded in 1269 by the rich and powerful combined Guild of the Holy Cross, the Blessed Virgin and St John the Baptist. The tower seems almost too small for the nave, lit by a series of tall windows. Over the chancel arch are the remains of what must have been a spectacular wall painting of the Last Judgement, whitewashed over in the course of the Reformation, and rediscovered only in the 19th century. The chapel is used nowadays by the neighbouring Grammar School, partly accommodated in the Guildhall, a superb timber-framed building dating from the early part of the 15th century. In Shakespeare's time the lower of its two halls was much used by visiting troupes of actors, and it's more than likely that the young William would have had his imagination stirred by their performances.

21

Timber-framing continues along this side of Church Street with the wonderfully intact **Almshouses**, a 150-ft (45m) long terrace still in use for its original purpose. On the opposite side, most of the buildings are in brick, among them Mason Croft, a fine early 18th-century house which once belonged to Marie Corelli. Accompanied by her Belgian companion, Berta Vyver, this immensely popular novelist of the day came to Stratford in 1899, and set about establishing herself as the high priestess of the Shakespeare Cult. Her pretension and indulgence in eccentricities such as driving around the town in a miniature carriage drawn by Shetland ponies named Puck and Ariel or drifting along the Avon in a gondola poled by an authentic Venetian were tolerated for a while, but by the time she died in 1924 she had been largely forgotten.

Church Street: the Guild Chapel and Almhouses

Hall's Croft

The end of Church Street marks the boundary between the ancient village of Stradforde and the new town laid out at the end of the 12th century. The street bearing left towards the parish church, the focal point of the older settlement, is appropriately named Old Town. It passes ★ **Hall's Croft** ❻ (late March to late October Monday to Saturday 9.30am–5pm, Sunday 10am–5pm, winter Monday to Saturday 10am–4pm, Sunday 10.30am–4pm), the home of Shakespeare's daughter Susanna and her husband, Dr John Hall. The couple lived here until Shakespeare's death in 1616, when they moved into New Place.

Bought by the Birthplace Trust in 1949, it is a fine, three-storeyed structure, the upper two overhanging. Begun at the start of the 16th century, the house was much enlarged by Dr Hall, a prosperous physician. His 'consulting room' is on view, and there is an exhibition on the medicine of Shakespeare's time, as well as fine examples of period furniture. The walled garden is full of atmosphere.

The Saxon monastery of Stratford probably stood on the same site as ★★ **Holy Trinity Church** ❼. Approached via an avenue of lime trees, the church is one of the finest parish churches in the Midlands, dating mostly from the early 14th century and the late 15th century, and is well worth a visit for its own sake. However, most visitors undertake the longish walk from the town centre in order to pay homage at **Shakespeare's grave** (March to October, Monday to Saturday 8.30am–6pm, Sunday 2–7pm; November to February, Monday to Saturday, 8.30am–4pm, Sunday 2–5pm) in the chancel. His remains lie beneath a simple gravestone with the famous, definitely sub-Shakespearean inscription:

Holy Trinity Church

22

> Good frend for Iesvs sake forbeare,
> To digg the dust enclosed heare;
> Bleste be ye man y spares thes stones,
> And cvrst be he yt moves my bones.

On the north wall is the famous bust, the work of Gerard Johnson, placed here by the family not long after Shakespeare's death. It may therefore be a reasonable likeness, despite the view of one commentator that it makes the playwright look like a 'self-satisfied schoolmaster'. The graves of Anne Hathaway and other members of the family are also here, and in the chapel named after him, among other Clopton tombs, is the much-restored cenotaph of Hugh Clopton, whose body rests in London.

Brass Rubbing Centre

The riverside parkland is reached from an opening off Old Town. In the park, an old orangery has been converted into the **Brass Rubbing Centre** (daily, 10am–6pm in summer, 11am–5pm winter), where visitors can admire a range of brasses and make rubbings of their choice. A little ferry conveys passengers to and from the far bank of the Avon.

Dominating the far end of the parkland is the great mass of the ★★★ **Royal Shakespeare Theatre** ❽ (RSC collection and backstage area tours at 1.30pm and 5.30pm dependent on play schedules, more frequently on Sunday). This world-renowned institution dates from 1879, following previous unsuccessful attempts to create a permanent Shakespeare Theatre in the town of his birth. The original building was in a style described as a hybrid between French château and Rhineland castle, with a highly romantic outline of towers, turrets and dormer windows. Following a fire in 1926, a new theatre was commissioned

Royal Shakespeare Theatre

from a young and unknown architect, Elisabeth Whitworth Scott. Though severe and bulky, her building fulfilled its brief admirably in functional terms. The interior has marvellous Art Deco fittings. Of the original building, the art gallery and library survived the fire and the **Swan Theatre**, a modern interpretation of a galleried auditorium of Shakespeare's time, has been cleverly fitted into the drum-like walls of the original theatre.

Anne Hathaway's Cottage

23

Still not quite swallowed up by Stratford's suburbs is the hamlet of Shottery, famous as the location of ★★★ **Anne Hathaway's Cottage ❾** (late March to late October Monday to Saturday 9am–5pm, Sunday 9.30am– 5pm, winter Monday to Saturday 9.30am–4pm, Sunday 10am–4pm), the most irresistibly picturesque of all the Shakespeare houses. Only a mile or so from the town centre, it can be reached on foot, perhaps following in the footsteps of young William as he set off to woo his bride to be. But most visitors nowadays come by car or open-top bus.

The Hathaway Bedstead

The subject of countless postcards and picture-books, the timber-framed home of Shakespeare's wife-to-be crouches beneath its luxuriant thatch. Its almost overwhelming charm is compounded by the large cottage garden through which it is approached, though this is modelled on romantic 19th-century ideas on what such a garden should look like rather than on the working farmyard which it would have been in Anne's day. Anne was born around 1555, some eight years earlier than William; by the time of their marriage in 1582 she was already three months pregnant. Her house stayed in the family until 1892, when it was bought by the Birthplace Trust. The presence of original items of furniture adds immeasurably to the atmosphere of the place. Beyond the house is an orchard and a recently laid out Shakespeare Tree Garden, planted with most of the trees mentioned in the plays.

Lord Leycester's Hospital

Route 2

Warwick, Leamington and Kenilworth

Jousting at the castle

One of the most delightful old towns of Midland England with a wealth of late medieval and Georgian buildings, **Warwick** is built on a rise above the Avon. From much of the surrounding countryside the town seems to be dominated by the majestic tower of St Mary's Church, but it is above all the great castle – often described as England's finest medieval stronghold – on its rocky bluff overlooking the Avon that draws visitors here in great numbers.

Warwick's origins go back to Saxon times, when, in the second decade of the 10th century, Ethelfleda, the Queen of Mercia and a daughter of King Alfred, laid out a settlement and built a fortification. This first stronghold almost certainly underlies the base of the great motte built on the orders of William the Conqueror which forms part of the defences of the present castle and which is known as Ethelfleda's Mound. The town seems to have flourished under the protection of the castle and its lords, great magnates with a major influence on the course of English history. Built of timber and thatch like most medieval towns, Warwick was as vulnerable to fire as any of them, especially after a dry summer, and on 5 September 1694 a great conflagration consumed much of the area within the old walls, including the nave of St Mary's. Rebuilding took place in a harmonious style, with use of brick and of the local attractive but rather soft sandstone, making an agreeable contrast with the surviving timber-framed buildings.

The basic layout of the town is that of a cross formed by High Street, Church Street, Jury Street and Castle Street. Their meeting point, once the site of a market cross, is marked by substantial edifices all dating from the time of the town's rebuilding. The **Court House** ❶ of 1725 whose ground floor is occupied by the Tourist Information Centre was designed by Francis Smith, master builder and twice Mayor of Warwick. The building also houses the Town Museum and the Warwickshire Yeomanry Museum.

Lined with dignified Georgian buildings, the High Street leads to the 12th-century **West Gate** with its massive archway partly cut into the living rock. Atop it is St James' Chapel, which, together with the other buildings of ★★ **Lord Leycester's Hospital** ❷ (Summer, Tuesday to Saturday and Bank Holiday Mondays 10am–5.30pm, Winter 10am–4pm), forms one of the most picturesque, most photographed and most painted urban scenes in England. The splendidly irregular jetted and gabled buildings making up the Hospital are almshouses, still the home of a community of ex-servicemen.

The institution was founded in 1571 by Robert Dudley, Earl of Leicester, supposedly the lover of Queen Elizabeth

Lord Leycester's Hospital: Master's House detail

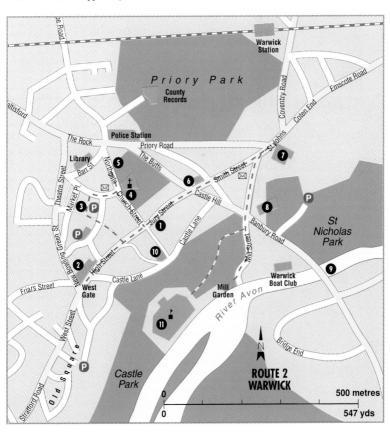

ROUTE 2
WARWICK

I, as a home for old soldiers. Some of the buildings are of even earlier date, since some of the town's guilds had their headquarters here as far back as 1383.

An archway leads to a quadrangle whose charm is partly due to the elaborate Master's House, a convincing Victorian attempt to be more medieval than the Middle Ages, decorated with some of the many heraldic bears to be seen in the town. The galleried wing is, however, authentically ancient. Steps lead up to the gallery and the magnificent mid-15th century **Guildhall**, off which is the Chaplains' Dining Hall housing the Museum of the Queen's Own Hussars. Equally striking, entered at ground level, is the Great Hall with its sturdy roof structure. **St James' Chapel** is approached via steps and a passageway between buttresses, high above the traffic and giving a good view of the timber-framed houses opposite and of pretty West Street stretching away towards Charlecote. Lit by a 15th-century candelabrum, the Chapel was begun in the 14th century and, despite being extensively restored and altered in the 19th century, is full of atmosphere. A passageway leads to the rear of the Hospital where the double-jettied building known as the Malt House has a complex and attractive pattern of timber decoration. Beyond is the restored **Master's Garden**, set within old walls.

Modern life in Warwick centres on the area around the Market Place with its fine stone-built **Market Hall ❸** of 1670. The building, its arches now blocked in with windows, is now the home of the **Warwickshire Museum** (Monday to Saturday 10am–5pm, summer Sundays 2–5pm). Visitors should not be deterred by the guardian of the place, the biggest of all the many bears to be seen around the town. The museum has displays on local archaeology, geology, geography and ecology as well as a

The Market Hall

Lord Leycester's Hospital: in the Master's Garden

model of the town as it was before the great fire. But the most striking of all the exhibits is the splendid mid-16th century **Sheldon tapestry map** of Warwickshire which, among countless intriguing details, brings out the dramatic contrast between the wooded Arden and open Feldon areas of the county.

Sheldon tapestry map

On the east side of the Market Place is the building known as the Tilted Wig, which in the 18th century housed the butchers' market beneath what were then open arches. Opposite is **Abbotsford**, a fine town mansion of 1714 built by Francis Smith in the local stone which proved so unreliable that the building had to be completely refaced in the 1960s. It's partnered by modern county council offices.

The tower of ★ **St Mary's Church**  rises above the roadway. The tower, 174ft (53m) high, can be climbed, the reward being an superb view of the town and castle in their green Warwickshire setting. The church is the glory of the town, despite the rebuilding of nave and tower after the fire. The spacious impression given by the nave is due to the generous dimensions of the windows and the height of the aisles, equal to that of the nave itself.

Ambrose Dudley tomb and the Beauchamp Chapel

Spared by the fire were the Norman crypt with its massive columns, the Dean's Chapel with lovely fan vaulting, the 14th-century chancel, and the ★★ **Beauchamp Chapel**. Completed in 1464, the sumptuous Chapel is one of the most evocative burial places in England, with the tombs of Richard Beauchamp, Ambrose Dudley and Robert Dudley, Earl of Leicester and founder of the hospital named after him. The gilded **brass effigy of Richard Beauchamp**, Earl of Warwick, was made some 15 years after his death in 1439 and is rightly famous. The great magnate lies with his head resting on a helmet, his hands raised in supplication. At his feet are a bear and a griffin; around the tomb are figures of weepers and angels.

Running north from the church, **Northgate Street**  has been described as 'the most handsome Georgian street in the Midlands'. The houses lining the right-hand side are fine enough, but opposite them stand the town's most imposing public buildings, the Shire Hall, rebuilt in the 1750s, and the severe County Gaol from the 1770s. The vista is closed by Northgate House, built in 1689 and consequently a survivor of the fire. Church Street, also lined with well-mannered houses from the period of reconstruction, descends towards its junction with High Street and Jury Street. The latter leads to the charming 15th-century **East Gate**  topped by a chapel dedicated to St Peter and now only used by pedestrians. Beyond is Smith Street. Close to the gate is the street's great ornament, the late 17th-century brick-built **Landor House**, birthplace of the Romantic poet Walter Savage Landor, while at the far end is **St John's** ❼. This fine early 17th-century stone building is the home of the some of the other collections of the **Warwickshire Museum** (Good Friday to late September, Friday, weekends and Bank Holidays 10am–1pm, 2–4pm), among them reconstructions of a Victorian classroom and kitchen. The Museum of the Royal Warwickshire Regiment shares the building. Its most famous soldier was Field Marshal Bernard Montgomery of Alamein; his famous beret is a prize exhibit.

St Nicholas' Church ❽, uninspiringly rebuilt in the late 18th and mid-19th centuries, overlooks the traffic hurrying to and from the Banbury direction across **Castle Bridge** ❾. This handsome 100-ft (30m) single-span structure was built in 1793 to replace the medieval bridge which brought traffic too close to the castle walls for comfort. Now a cul-de-sac, **Mill Street** completely escaped the effects of the fire and contains a fine array of timber-framed houses. At the far end there is a striking view of the Castle's Caesar's Tower high above. The **Mill Garden** is open to the public from spring to autumn.

The Castle can be approached via its Stable Block at the foot of Castle Street. One of the prettiest of the town's streets, Castle Street also has one of the prettiest houses in Warwick, a timber-framed early Elizabethan building named after its owner, Thomas Oken, a prosperous mercer and benefactor of the town. His home is now the delightful **Doll Museum** ❿ (Easter to late September Monday to Saturday 10am–5pm, Sunday 1–5pm, winter Saturdays until dusk), inhabited not only by dolls but also by other toys and games.

Every year, 750,000 visitors happily pay a substantial entrance fee to visit ★★★ **Warwick Castle** ⓫ (April to October 10am–6pm, November to March 10am–5pm), once described as 'the most perfect piece of castellated antiquity in the kingdom'. Most seem well satisfied; the castle has everything that could be expected: a wonderful site, great towers and walls, dungeons, sumptuous state rooms, and glorious grounds and gardens.

Few locations in the gentle countryside of Warwickshire offer the defensive possibilities of the sandstone spur above the Avon. The natural potential of the site has been fully exploited by successive owners and builders and there are few views more emblematic of England's historic heritage than that of Warwick's walls and towers rising above luxuriant parkland and reflected in the river.

The castle's history stretches over a period of more than 1,000 years, beginning with the fortification built by Ethelfleda. It was only two years after the Conquest, in 1068, that King William ordered the castle to be refounded, a standard Norman motte and bailey construc-

*Mill Street and Mill Garden with
Caesar's Tower*

Castle guard

Warwick Castle and the Avon

tion which was succeeded in the 12th and 13th centuries by a more permanent structure in stone. Much of the fabric of this castle was replaced in the mid-14th century by Thomas Beauchamp, Earl of Warwick, who built Caesar's Tower and the clock tower, while his son, another Thomas, was responsible for Guy's Tower.

The greatest of the castle's lords, Richard Neville, known to history as Warwick the Kingmaker (*see page 63*), seems to have been too preoccupied with national politics to devote time to architecture, but his successor, the Duke of Clarence, found time to build the north gate and start work on the Clarence Tower before being accused of high treason and meeting a horrible end, according to some sources and to Shakespeare, by being 'drowned in a butt of Malmsey'. For a while, the castle was in the hands of his brother, King Richard III.

Eventually it became the property of the Greville family, Fulke Greville being created Lord Brooke by James I in 1604. The eighth Lord Brooke was granted the title of Earl of Warwick in 1759. The Grevilles were responsible for the conversion of what had become a crumbling medieval fortress into what was subsequently admired as 'the most princely seat within the midland parts of the realm'. Walls and towers remain as reminders of medieval might, and basements, dungeons and undercroft preserve

Siege in progress

their ancient character, but the habitable part of the castle consists of a sumptuous series of state rooms of Jacobean and later date. In the 18th century, the grounds were lavishly re-landscaped by Capability Brown and extended north towards the new bridge across the Avon. In 1978, following sales of family heirlooms, the castle passed into the hands of Madame Tussaud's. The famous waxworks has subsequently further enhanced the castle's appeal to the crowds of visitors, particularly by animating the interior with a series of convincing historical tableaux.

Most visitors arrive via the extensive car and coach park reached from West Street, through the 18th-century **Stable Block**. From here a curving pathway makes a dramatic approach to the **gatehouse and barbican** with **Guy's Tower** rising up splendidly on the right to a height of 128ft (40m). Once within the great circuit of walls, the visitor has various choices. **The Armoury**, **Torture Chamber** and **Dungeon** beneath **Caesar's Tower** are understandably popular with children, but perhaps the best way to enter into the spirit of the castle's history is to descend into the vaulted underground chambers and passageways of the medieval castle and enjoy the elaborate and entertaining tableaux entitled 'Kingmaker'. This is a convincing evocation of the preparations which preceded the Battle of Barnet in 1471. Richard Neville lost both the battle and his life in this, one of the decisive encounters of the Wars of the Roses. As well as armourers and others at work, there are children larking about, a horse giving off a powerful stable smell, and living costumed figures barely distinguishable from their waxwork counterparts.

Guy's Tower

A very different epoch is evoked in the tableaux of the **Royal Weekend Party of 1898**. Towards the end of the 19th century, Warwick had become a great centre of social life, largely due to the influence of the Countess of Warwick, born Frances but universally known as Daisy. Among the guests populating some of the former private apartments are the young Winston Churchill, Field Marshal Lord Roberts, the future George V lighting a cigarette, and Edward Prince of Wales, a frequent visitor and rumoured lover of Daisy. From this part of the building there are dramatic views of the Avon far below.

Royal Weekend Party of 1898

The Chapel, Great Hall and State Rooms are reached by stairs. The early 17th-century **Chapel** has medieval stained glass and superbly carved wooded panels. The 18th-century Dining Room, designed by some of the era's master craftsmen, boasts splendidly framed royal portraits, including a famous study of Charles I on horseback. The **Great Hall** had to be rebuilt in the late 19th century after being damaged by fire, but still exudes the atmosphere of the Middle Ages with its displays of arms and armour. The **State Rooms** compete with each other in magnificence: the Red Drawing Room has bold red lacquer panelling; the Cedar Drawing Room a superb plaster ceiling; the Green Drawing Room of mementoes of the Civil War; the Queen Anne Bedroom a bed intended for that royal personage but never used; while the Blue Boudoir has a portrait after Holbein of Henry V.

The Great Hall

Next to the so-called **Ghost Tower** the great **mound** rises to a surprising height. Topped by mock fortifications, it offers a magnificent prospect over the castle grounds, the river, and the lush countryside beyond.

Royal Leamington Spa

Adjacent to Warwick and recently declared the most favoured place to live in Britain, ★ **Leamington Spa** has prided itself on its amenities since it began its development as a spa town in the late 18th century.

The focal point of the town is still the **Pump Room** by the bridge over the Leam. Built in 1814 and rebuilt in 1925 it retains its original colonnade, though the crowds who come here nowadays are more likely to be on their way to attend fitness classes than to be taking the waters. An essential part of the original 'cure' was the health-giving stroll, and to this end landscaped areas and walks were laid out along the river banks. To the east are the showpiece **Jephson Gardens**, named after Joseph Henry Jephson (1798–1878), the physician and philanthropist who contributed much to the town's reputation. Honoured with a statue housed within a little temple, he was referred to in his obituary as the 'Father of Leamington'.

The Pump Room

Jephson Gardens

To the south of the river is the older part of the town where most of the original springs were to be found. Here is the town's big Victorian All Saints Church as well as the ★ **Library and Art Gallery** (Monday and Tuesday, Thursday to Saturday 10am–1pm and 2–5pm, Thursday also 6–8pm), with a dignified domed interior. There are good displays on local history and the extensive and far from average art collection has been re-displayed to enhance its appeal to all visitors. The paintings include fine Flemish canvases as well as a representative selection of works by English 20th-century artists like L. S. Lowry, Graham Sutherland and Stanley Spencer.

31

By the second decade of the 19th century the developers of the expanding town turned their eyes on the unbuilt land to the north of the river, and it is here that most of the classically elegant architecture so characteristic of Leamington is to be found. Some of the finest building is to be found along **Newbold Terrace**; the corner building opposite the Pump Room with its double-decker porch is particularly striking. In complete contrast is the contemporary Royal Spa Centre with its cinema and theatre.

From the bridge the grand and slightly curving thoroughfare running northward is known as **The Parade**, a name expressive of the early 19th-century town's pretensions and social ambitions. Much of the Parade's original elegance has been preserved, especially on the upper floors above the modern shopfronts. A decisive interruption to Regency harmony occurred however when the assertive red brick and brown stone Victorian Town Hall was built in 1884. Once described as a 'mongrel palace, a Tudor/Baroque crossbreed with a bit of Islamic blood in the minaret', it's an extraordinarily ornate edifice, crammed with ornament and topped by a dome.

The Parade

Landsdowne Cresent

The Parade continues northwards towards Beauchamp Gardens, part of a grand development scheme of the 1820s that, like other local projects, was never completed. To the west of the Parade, Clarendon Square, its terraces interrupted by a villa or two on one side, provided a refuge for the future Emperor Napoleon III when he came here in 1838. But perhaps the most attractive urban compositions in Leamington are to the east; the superb curve of **Landsdowne Crescent** was built in 1835, while behind it is **Landsdowne Circus**, a sociable arrangement of delightful semi-detached villas. No 10 was the residence of the American writer Nathaniel Hawthorne who described it as 'his little nest' and wrote part of his *Our Old Home* there. Leamington has other literary associations; Dickens came here on more than one occasion, and parts of *Dombey and Son* are set in the town, among the 'deep shade of leafy trees'.

Kenilworth

Long shadows at Kenilworth

A pleasant town barely 4 miles (6km) to the north of Warwick, Kenilworth has a parish church with a fine Norman doorway probably taken from its once important priory. There are a number of attractive houses, black and white or Georgian brick, the prettiest buildings on Castle Green facing the splendid ruins of ★★ **Kenilworth Castle** (late March to late October 10am–6pm, November to late March 10am–4pm), the great stronghold which played a prominent role in the life of the nation and was covered in even greater glory when romanticised by Sir Walter Scott in his 1821 novel *Kenilworth*.

The castle was built on rising ground whose natural defences were strengthened by flooding much of the surrounding marshland. Despite centuries of neglect and deliberate destruction after the Civil War, Kenilworth re-

mains an evocative place, full of echoes of history which its owners, English Heritage, bring to life each summer with a programme of colourful events, many of them staged on the long causeway leading to the castle.

An outline of the architectural history of the Middle Ages and Tudor times can be read in the remaining structures, built in warm red sandstone which seems to glow in the light of late afternoon and evening. Though nothing is left of the early 12th-century timber fortress erected by the castle's first lord, Geoffrey de Clinton, the massive **Keep** built by his descendants later in the century still stands, an awesome monument to Norman might. The full 14-ft (4.3m) thickness of its walls is revealed by the breach made by Cromwell's men on the north side.

The 90-ft (27m) long **Great Hall** dates from the 14th century, one of the many additions to the castle made by John of Gaunt which turned it from a grim stronghold into one of the finest palaces of the realm. In 1563, Elizabeth I granted the castle to her favourite, Robert Dudley, later the Earl of Leicester, who added the gatehouse and apartments named after him and further transformed the castle into a residence fit for elaborate entertainments. In 1575, on the last of her visits, Elizabeth I was greeted by a 'Lady of the Lake' and accompanying nymphs aboard a torchlit vessel floating on the lake. It's thought that the 11-year-old Shakespeare may well have been taken to some of the lavish shows that filled her stay; Oberon's remarks in *A Midsummer Night's Dream* about hearing 'a mermaid on a dolphin's back, Uttering such dulcet and harmonious breath, That the rude sea grew civil at her song' seem to recall these glamorous days and nights.

33

Great Hall window and Robert Dudley

Kenilworth had, of course, known sterner events. After their defeat at the battle of Lewes in 1264, the king and his son Prince Edward were brought here by the castle's lord, Simon de Montfort. In a reversal of fortune, Edward escaped and raised an army, returning to Kenilworth where he confronted de Montfort's son, who barely escaped with his life by swimming the lake. After the defeat and death of the elder de Montfort at the battle of Evesham, Edward once more came to Kenilworth, putting the castle to a nine-month siege which was raised only when the defenders succumbed to starvation.

Half a century later, the unfortunate Edward II had cause to hear the name of Kenilworth with dismay, since it was near here, on Blacklow Hill, that his lover, Piers Gaveston, was beheaded by the Earl of Warwick. In 1326 it was to Kenilworth Castle that Edward was brought by his estranged wife Isabella and forced to abdicate in favour of his son, and it was from here that he departed to meet his death at the hands of his murderers in Berkeley Castle.

Route 3

Into Arden

Mary Arden's House

Young falconer at the Countryside Museum

Stratford – Wilmcote – Henley-in-Arden – Packwood House and Baddesley Clinton – Hatton – Charlecote Park – Stratford (43 miles/ 69km)

Three miles (5km) northwest of Stratford, **Wilmcote** can be reached on foot along the towpath of the Stratford Canal or by car by a turning off the A3400. The village has a beautiful Victorian Gothic church, but it is the presence here of ★★ **Mary Arden's House**, the farmstead which was almost certainly the home of Shakespeare's mother (late March to late October, daily 9.30am–5pm, Sunday 10am–5pm; otherwise 10am–4pm, Sunday 10.30am–4pm), that brings a continuous stream of visitors.

An old Warwickshire family, the Ardens were prosperous yeomen farmers who built this fine half-timbered structure in the early 16th century. In 1557, Mary Arden, one of eight daughters, married John Shakespeare, the son of Richard Shakespeare of Snitterfield who was a tenant of her father. The house was subsequently mortgaged, and all William Shakespeare's later attempts to recover his mother's ancestral home were in vain. The property continued in use as a working farm until the early 20th century. The house itself is furnished throughout with authentic pieces, while the farmyard and its outbuildings have found a new use as an excellent rural museum, the **Shakespeare Countryside Museum**. The house is a text-

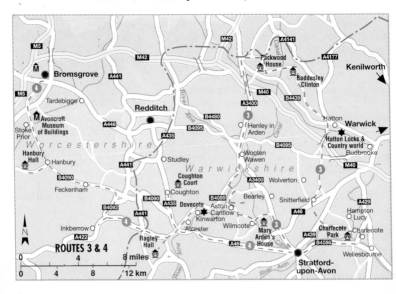

ROUTES 3 & 4

book example of the use of Midland oak, with ancient beams still carrying the marks of the axes which formed them. There are time-worn stone flags on the ground floor while upstairs floorboards rise and fall in a disconcertingly drunken fashion. The farm has a dovecote, a cider mill, a blacksmith's, and agricultural implements.

Two miles (3.5km) away across the fields on the banks of the little River Alne is **Aston Cantlow** with a fine black and white pub next to an equally picturesque late medieval structure known as the Guildhall. It is more than likely that Mary Arden was baptised in the church here, and tradition has it was here that she and John Shakespeare were married, though parish records only begin a few years later.

Aston Cantlow

A minor road crosses the Alne to join the B4089 northward to **Wootton Wawen**. Standing in pretty parkland, 17th-century Wootton Hall was the home of the Prince Regent's Mrs Fitzherbert. The parish church has been described as 'an epitome in stone of the history of the Church of England' and does indeed have fine features from most periods, from the sturdy Saxon base of the tower to the Perpendicular windows and battlements of the nave.

35

A short drive along the A3400 leads to ★ **Henley-in-Arden**, its long main street a continuous display of listed buildings dating from medieval times onwards. Henley was once dominated by the castle of Beaudesert on the far bank of the Alne, here little more than a stream. Only the earthen mound on which the castle was built has survived, but Henley has continued to flourish, its position on one of the main roads between London, Stratford and Birmingham a guarantee of prosperity.

Henley-in-Arden: the Guildhall

Nowadays there's little sign of the disreputable behaviour which once caused it to be denounced as the gathering-place of 'loose people' engaged in 'Morris Dances and other heathenish customs'. Among the array of fine old buildings in timber, brick and stone there are numerous coaching inns which once served the needs of travellers using the turnpike road, but the outstanding structure, next to the parish church, is the 15th-century timber-framed **Guildhall** with its first floor hall and numerous relics of the guild and court that met here. The old market cross stands nearby. Across the Alne is Beaudesert's **St Nicholas**, the very picture of a country church.

To the north, across the M40 via the A3400 and along a minor road to the right, is ★★ **Packwood House** (National Trust; late March to end September, Wednesday to Sunday and Bank Holiday Monday, 2pm to 6pm, garden 1.30pm to 6pm), a fine timber-framed dwelling begun in the 16th century and with one of the most remarkable gardens in England. Wearing a coat of rendering, the house

Packwood House sundial

Packwood's Yew Garden

has been extended considerably over time. Its many-gabled outline is extremely picturesque. The interior houses a fascinating collection of 16th-century furniture and tapestries. Outside, the formal Carolean garden has gazebos in each of its four corners; a raised terrace gives access to the extraordinary sight of the famous Victorian ★★ **Yew Garden**. The conical clipped yews represent the Sermon on the Mount, with groups of disciples and the four Evangelists, while the mushroom-headed yew on the mount stands for Christ Himself.

From Packwood, lanes lead eastward across the Stratford and Grand Union Canals to one of the most delightful moated manor houses in the country. In its romantic setting, ★★ **Baddesley Clinton** (National Trust; March, April and October 1.30–5pm, May to Septmber 1.30–5.30pm Wednesday to Sunday) dates from the 14th century, though it was much added to subsequently. The grey stone building with its battlements and formidable porch is approached by an ancient bridge, a replacement for the original drawbridge. Inside, there are many fascinating details including fine fireplaces, heraldic stained glass and family portraits. There is a private chapel and a priest's hole built by the specialist Nicholas Owen. In the 15th century the owner of Baddesley Clinton was one Nicholas Brome, a vengeful character who amongst other misdemeanours is supposed to have slain a priest for tickling his wife under her chin. In expiation of this offence he built a handsome tower for the nearby parish church.

36

Baddesley Clinton

About 5 miles (8km) southeast of Baddesley Clinton, via narrow lanes or the A4177, are ★ **Hatton Locks**, which raise boats travelling on the Grand Union Canal a total height of 146ft (45m) from the valley of the Avon to the raised land of the Birmingham plateau. The 21 locks stretching over 2 miles (3.5km) are the longest feature of their kind on the Grand Union and were part of a modernisation scheme carried out in the 1920s and '30s in an attempt to make the canal navigable for barges much wider than traditional narrowboats. Sometimes called the 'Stairway to Heaven', the locks are linked by a nature trail to **Hatton Country World**, a busy attraction which boasts a farm park amongst its craft shops and factory outlets.

Hatton Country World

The lanes winding through the countryside south of Hatton provide an alternative to entanglement in the traffic racing along the A46. The village of **Snitterfield** is proud of its Shakespearean connections. Richard Shakespeare was a resident, dying here in 1560; one of his two sons, Henry, continued to farm here, while John moved to Stratford, later becoming the father of William. **Hampton Lucy** with its iron bridge over the Avon reflects early 19th-century taste with model cottages and an early Gothic Revival church of great character.

A fitting climax to this tour of quintessential Warwickshire is reached at ★★ **Charlecote Park** (National Trust; April to October Friday to Tuesday 11am–6pm, house closed 1–2pm), the domain of the Lucy family since the mid-13th century.

Their original home, a manor house close to the confluence of the Avon and the little River Dene, was demolished in 1558 by Sir Thomas Lucy and replaced by a stately Tudor residence, E-shaped in honour of his Queen, Elizabeth I. The delightful gatehouse in mellow local brick is entirely of this time, whereas the house itself was largely reconstructed in the mid-19th century by George Hammond Lucy and his wife Mary Elizabeth.

The interior is a faithful reflection of their romantic sensibility; as well as family portraits and wonderful stained glass, there is a fantastic Italian Renaissance *pietra dura* table and an extraordinary carved sideboard, the 'Charlecote Buffet', intended for Queen Victoria. The glorious parkland laid out around the meeting of the two rivers was landscaped by Capability Brown in 1760.

Enclosed by an ancient split-oak palisade, the park has a herd of Jacob sheep as well as red and fallow deer. A long-standing tradition had it that the young Shakespeare was caught poaching deer from the park; hauled before the local magistrate, who happened to be Sir Thomas Lucy, William's humiliation was such that he quit Stratford for London, where he caricatured Sir Thomas as Justice Shallow in the *Merry Wives of Windsor*. Unfortunately, there seems to be no truth in the tale, despite the familiarity with the poacher's skills expressed in such lines as:

What, hast not thou full often struck a doe,
And borne her cleanly by the keeper's nose?
(Titus Andronicus)

The B4086 follows the Avon back to Stratford.

Fallow deer at Charlecote Park

37

Charlecote gatehouse

Guarding the entrance

Alcester

Route 4

Westwards to Bromsgrove

Stratford –Alcester (Ragley Hall, Coughton Court) – Inkberrow – Feckenham – Hanbury Hall – Bromsgrove (41 miles/66km) *See map on page 34*

Alcester: Town Hall detail

Situated just off the A46, 8 miles (12km) west of Stratford, its centre relieved of through traffic, ★ **Alcester** can be enjoyed as one of the most attractive small towns in the Midlands. The town is a Roman foundation, located at a convenient point at the junction of roads and rivers; the great Roman highway of Ryknild Street linking Chester and Cirencester still forms the main road north, while the combined waters of the Arrow and Alne flow into the Avon about 4 miles (6.5km) downstream from the town.

A delightful jumble of old buildings in brick, stucco and timber jostle for position in the medieval town centre around the parish church and the early 17th-century **Town Hall**, its arches long since blocked in. The **church** has a fine pinnacled and battlemented tower dating from the 14th century, but the body was rebuilt around 1730 following a disastrous fire, the exterior in an appropriately Gothic style, the interior Classical. The monuments include a reclining figure of the Marquess of Hertford (died 1828) of nearby Ragley Hall and 16th-century alabaster effigies of Sir Fulke Greville and his wife, the latter with her under-garment being nibbled by the hound at her feet.

The church tower

Alcester's most photographed street is undoubtedly ★ **Malt Mill Lane** which runs gently downhill from the churchyard towards the river and has won a number of conservation awards; its houses, half-timbered or brick, date from late medieval times onwards.

From the centre of town it is just over a mile (2km) northeastwards along the B4089 to the scattered village of **Kinwarton** where a little medieval church and its 18th-century rectory make a pleasant group. Close by is an exceptionally fine circular ★ **dovecote** (April to October 9am–6pm or sunset if earlier, other times by prior appointment). Dating from the 14th century, it has some 600 nesting places as well as an original potence, the revolving post and ladder which enabled the nests to be reached.

The dovecote at Kinwarton

In the immediate vicinity of Alcester are two outstanding country houses. On a prominent rise 2 miles (3.5km) to the southwest of the town and overlooking the valley of the Arrow stands ★★ **Ragley Hall** (late March to early October Thursday to Sunday 11am–5pm), one of the finest stately homes in the Midlands and one of the most visited. For long the home of the Marquesses of Hertford, Ragley was begun around 1680, possibly on the site of an earlier house. In the early 19th century the east front was embellished by a great portico designed by Wyatt, while the west front remains in its original state.

Long neglected and used as a hospital in World War II, the house has undergone a lengthy and restoration in recent years. The 70-ft (21m) **Great Hall** is a stunning space, reaching up to the full height of the house and with magnificent plasterwork by James Gibbs. Other rooms include the Green Drawing Room and the **Red Saloon** with its wall coverings in silk. There are fine furnishings and paintings, but perhaps the most striking feature is the decoration of the south staircase hall; carried out between 1969 and 1983 by Graham Rust, it shows members of the family in a *trompe l'oeil* setting. The house stands in extensive parklands which were landscaped by Capability Brown in the mid-18th century. There's a rose garden, a maze, plenty of places to picnic, boating on the lake, an adventure wood and a self-guided countryside trail.

39

Ragley's Red Saloon

A short 2-mile (3.5km) drive along the A435 north from Alcester leads to **Coughton**. The village has two churches, both with close links to the Throckmorton family, long-standing occupants of the adjacent ★★ **Coughton Court** (National Trust; Mid-March to April Saturday and Sunday noon–5pm, May to late September Saturday to Wednesday noon–5pm, October Saturday and Sunday noon–5pm, Bank Holiday Mondays noon–5pm). There's a fine array of Throckmorton tombs in the parish church, while the Roman Catholic church is a reminder of the family's adherence to their faith. The Throckmortons came into possession of Coughton Court in 1409 and have lived here ever since.

Coughton Court

Coughton and the Throckmortons played a prominent part in the troubled course of English history during the Reformation and after. In 1583 the Throckmorton Plot

Coughton's gatehouse

aimed to put Mary Queen of Scots on to throne in place of Elizabeth. A few years later, in 1605, the house served as mission control for another frustrated conspiracy, the attempt by Guy Fawkes to blow the government skyhigh by exploding barrels of gunpowder concealed in the cellars of the Houses of Parliament. In the Civil War, Coughton was captured by Parliamentary forces, then bombarded and sacked by the Royalists. Later still, in 1688, an anti-Catholic mob swarmed up the road from Alcester and destroyed the east wing, thus opening up what had been an enclosed courtyard.

The imposing gatehouse with its array of windows, turrets and battlements, dates from the early 16th century. To either side are wings with charming late 18th-century Gothic windows, while beyond is a courtyard flanked by ranges of splendidly half-timbered buildings. The interior of the house is fascinating, being furnished with memorabilia of its long occupancy by a single family. Among the portraits is a fine 18th-century study of Sir Robert Throckmorton by Largillière, while the chemise worn by Mary Queen of Scots is particularly evocative. The priest's hiding place is one of many built by Nicholas Owen. The 25 acres (10 hectares) of grounds leading down to the little River Arrow include formal areas contrasting with the controlled luxuriance of a bog garden and an ambitious new garden set within ancient walls.

Six miles (10km) west of Alcester astride the A422 Worcester road is the village of **Inkberrow**, a pleasant enough place with fine old houses in brick and timber as well as more modern development. The brick Bull's Head

The Old Bull at Inkberrow

faces the timber-framed Old Bull across the little village green. The Old Bull has a double claim to fame: in 1582 Shakespeare is reputed to have stayed there, while more recently (relatively speaking) it has been the model for the inn at Ambridge in the BBC's imperishable radio soap opera *The Archers*. Fans may wish to pay tribute and check whether pub and village correspond to the picture of Middle England built up over the years.

For those less in thrall to the Bard and the BBC, Inkberrow can be bypassed by driving north on A441 and turning left on to the B4090 towards Droitwich and Bromsgrove (from Inkberrow return towards Alcester on A422, turning left on to the B4092 and left again along a minor road). The B4090 originated in a Roman road, the Salt Way, running east from Droitwich through the once extensive Feckenham Forest of which only scattered clumps remain. ★ **Feckenham** itself is a large and urbane village, with humble cottages and proud Georgian houses lining the main road, the High Street, and clustering around the green known as The Square.

A mile or so off the B4091 towards Bromsgrove is ★★ **Hanbury Hall** (National Trust; late March to late October 2–6pm). A perfectly composed red brick house of 1701 in William and Mary style, it was described at the time as 'a stately seate, meete for a Kinge's pallace' and has hardly been altered since. The interior has wall and ceiling paintings of great virtuosity by Sir James Thornhill, better known for the magnificent Painted Hall at Greenwich. As well as other paintings, there's an outstanding porcelain collection and an early 18th-century bed with all its original hangings. In the grounds is a large and finely ornamented orangery of about 1740 and a well-preserved ice house. The gardens were originally laid out in formal fashion by George Loudon. His Dutch-style parterres and enclosures were swept away in the later 18th-century fad for naturalistic landscaping, but are now being restored. Hanbury was built for a barrister member of the Vernon family, whose monuments fill the chancel of the **parish church** perched on the nearby hilltop.

Hanbury Hall

On the outskirts of Bromsgrove at Stoke Prior is the major open-air museum of the Midlands, the ★★ **Avoncroft Museum of Buildings** (April to May and September to October 11am–5pm, June to August 11am to 5.30pm, March and November 10.30am–4pm; closed Monday and Friday). Since 1967 a steadily growing number of historic structures have been carefully dismantled and re-erected here to give as complete a picture as possible of traditional buildings, the techniques used to construct them, and the activities that went on in them. As well as the 15th- and 16th-century timber-framed houses so characteristic of the region, there are oddities like a cockpit, a toll-house, and a lock-up. The working windmill, a post mill from Danzey Green in the Forest of Arden, is particularly popular. Less traditional is the 1946 prefab. Avoncroft is also the home of the **National Telephone Kiosk Collection**, which includes the classic police call-box which became the time-travelling Tardis in television's *Dr Who*.

Emergency calls at Avoncroft

Separated from Birmingham, 15 miles (24km) to the north, by the leafy barrier of the Lickey Hills, the old town of **Bromsgrove** is a favoured place for commuters to the Midland capital. Its once famous nail-making industry is remembered in the local **Museum** (Monday to Saturday 9.30am–5pm, Sunday 2–5pm), which also has good displays on the arts and crafts association which flourished at the start of the 20th century and was known as the Bromsgrove Guild. Skirting the town is the **Worcester and Birmingham Canal**. Opened in 1815, it burrows through a ridge of red sandstone in the 1,740-ft (530m) long Tardebigge Tunnel and overcomes the 259-ft (80m) drop to the Severn by means of the longest flight of navigable **locks** in the country, 36 in all.

Route 5

Southeast from Stratford

Stratford – Shipston-on-Stour – Upton House – Edge Hill – Farnborough – Gaydon – Wellesbourne – Stratford (43 miles/69km) *See map on pages 44–5*

Just to the south of Stratford, the B4632 leaves the A3400, crosses the little River Stour and enters ★ **Clifford Chambers**. The most attractive part of the village is around the church, where the old houses include an exceptionally fine rectory. In Shakespeare's time this 16th-century half-timbered building belonged to a John Shakespeare, who may well have been a relative. The large manor house of about 1700 was largely rebuilt by the great early 20th-century architect, Edwin Lutyens. In Shakespeare's day it was a favourite retreat of the poet Michael Drayton.

Other pretty villages accompany the Stour as its follows its leisurely course towards the Avon. Tiny **Atherstone-on-Stour** seems a world away from the sophistication of Stratford while **Preston-on-Stour** around its sloping green has a church partly rebuilt in 18th-century Gothic taste by James West, fomer owner of nearby **Alscot Park** (private). **Wimpstone** boasts a large ornamental fish farm and lily gardens, while ★ **Ilmington**, reached by a minor road running to the south, has all the pleasant characteristics of a Cotswold village. Old houses with mellow stone walls stand around the two greens, while the church has a sturdy Norman tower. To the southwest, Ilmington Downs form the highest point in Warwickshire (854ft/260m).

Ilmington

Shipston-on-Stour

Lanes lead to the old market town of **Shipston-on-Stour** 4 miles (6.5km) to the southeast, crossing the Roman Foss Way en route. Shipston bestrides the old main road linking Oxford with Stratford and Birmingham, and is still a busy place, though nowadays much heavy traffic mercifully finds the M40 motorway more convenient. Evidence of the little town's past importance includes stately coaching inns and a varied, mostly Georgian townscape in brick, stucco and the local grey stone. There's no trace of the horse tramway which once conveyed goods and passengers along its jolting course between here and Stratford.

A mile and a half (2.5km) to the north of Shipston is **Honington**, another in the series of charming Stour-side villages, reached off the A3400 across a five-arched late 17th-century bridge. The church kept its medieval tower when it was otherwise entirely rebuilt in classical style in the mid-17th century. Inside is a particularly grandiloquent monument to Sir Henry Parker, the prosperous London merchant who in 1685 spent part of his accumulated wealth on building handsome ★ **Honington Hall** (June to August, Wednesday and Bank Holiday Mondays, 2.30–5pm), an excellent example of a house of the period. The brick exterior is relatively sober, while the interior has sumptuous stucco decoration. The finest room is the Octagonal Saloon with a coffered dome.

Just over half a mile south of Honington, a long and narrow lane runs roughly eastward towards the two Tysoes, Upper and Middle. About a mile short of Upper Tysoe an old windmill can be seen crowning a hilltop to the right. In the romantic setting of the dell below the hill nestles **Compton Wynyates**, one of England's most alluring Tudor country houses, now firmly barred to the public. There are glimpses of this gloriously picturesque mellow brick building from the lane which winds up to the top of the escarpment, though a shaven lawn has now replaced the fantastical topiary garden which once formed an enchanting foreground to the south front of the house. A closer look at the house can be obtained from the end of the mile-long path leading over the flank of Windmill Hill from Upper Tysoe. But be warned: the path is a cul-de-sac – not even the chapel in the grounds is accessible.

Compton Wynyates

43

Beyond the Tysoes, the minor road joins the A422 from Banbury to Stratford. A mile or so to the east, beyond the steep rise up the escarpment, is ★★ **Upton House** (National Trust; late March to October Saturday to Wednesday 2–6pm). Solidly classical in appearance, Upton was built in 1695, probably on the site of an earlier house, for Sir Rushout Cullen, then much modified in the early 20th century by Viscount Bearstead, a member of the Shell dynasty, who filled it with an extraordinarily rich collection of paintings and porcelain. The British pictures include works by Reynolds, Romney, Lawrence and Raeburn as well as by Gainsborough and Hogarth, but the great

Upton House gardens

strength of the collection lies in its superb Dutch and Flemish paintings, among them canvases by van de Weyden, van der Goes, Bosch and Breughel, Rubens, Ruysdael and Jan Steen. There are also pictures by Italian masters including Tintoretto, and a wonderful El Greco, *The Stripping of Christ.* As well as Chelsea and Sèvres porcelain, there are Brussels tapestries and 18th-century furniture.

The extensive gardens make ingenious use of the sloping site and of a deep coombe. There are terraces, rockeries, pools which date back to the original Dutch-style landscaping of the late 17th century, a modern water garden, the national aster collection, and a kitchen garden.

From the A422 a lane runs along the top of **Edge Hill**, a famous name in English history since it was here, on 23 October 1642, that the first, albeit inconclusive battle of the Civil War was fought. A castellated tower (now 'The Castle' pub, *see page 63*), built by Sanderson Miller around 1750, marks the spot where the King set up his standard. The Royalist army was deployed along the ridge to face the Parliamentary forces of the Earl of Essex advancing from the village of Kineton across what was then

Edge Hill: the tower

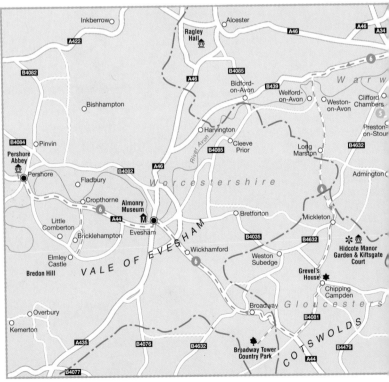

un-hedged, open country below. Impatient for success, the King's cavalry charged their enemy on both flanks, forcing many of them to flee. Preferring the pleasures of the pursuit, Prince Rupert and his cavalrymen ignored the opportunity to attack the Parliamentary centre from the rear and raced as far as Kineton, where they came up against sterner resistance led by John Hampden. In the meantime, the remaining Parliamentarians, among them a young captain called Oliver Cromwell, had advanced and captured the royal standard, though it was later recovered. Judging that the situation was too chaotic to be redeemed, Essex ordered his forces to retreat to Coventry while the King, claiming victory, continued towards London.

At the foot of the hill is the village of **Radway**, with attractive houses in the distinctive local ironstone, the colour of demerara sugar. An ancient building which had once belonged to the monks of Stoneleigh Abbey became the residence of the Miller family in the early 18th century. It was Gothicised by Sanderson Miller, among whose friends was the novelist Henry Fielding, who treated his host to a pre-publication reading of *Tom Jones* here. Radway's church has Renaissance glass and monuments

Radway church

45

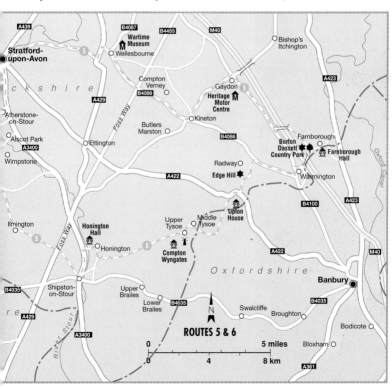

ROUTES 5 & 6

to the Miller family and to Captain Kingswell, a Royalist soldier who fell in the Battle of Edge Hill. Further victims of the battle are buried at **Warmington**, another attractive village 3 miles (5km) east of Edge Hill.

Lanes lead 2 miles (3.5km) northeast, across the M40, to Farnborough, whose glory is ★ **Farnborough Hall** (National Trust; April to September Wednesday to Saturday 2–6pm, terrace walk only Thursday and Friday as well). In the 14th century, the manor of Farnborough was in the ownership of John Raleigh, an ancestor of the more famous Sir Walter. In 1683 it came into the possession of the Holbech family who have lived here ever since. The house, a symmetrical composition in warm brown ironstone with grey stone dressings, is set in a fine landscape which has been described as 'not so much a garden, more a country walk'. The great terrace winds for half a mile, passing little temples and ending in an obelisk. It is thought to have been planned to connect with a similar terrace extending out from Mollington, another Holbech property.

Burton Dassett beacon and church

A lane leads northwest from Farnborough to **Burton Dassett**, where the rolling hills have been turned into a Country Park. The hilltop beacon was erected in the 14th century, probably to commemorate the abandonment of Burton Dassett village and its conversion by the Spencer family into a great sheep ranch. Such lost villages are common in this part of Warwickshire, where a peasant population decimated by the Black Death was in no position to resist the 'rationalisation' proposed by powerful landowners. The former importance of the village can be gauged by the great size of its church, which survived. Inside, the floor rises with the hillside, and there is much entertaining medieval carving.

Back across the M40, the B4100 leads to the old airfield at Gaydon which is now the home of the ★★ **Heritage Motor Centre** (April to October 10am–6pm, November to March 10am–4.30pm) with the world's largest collection of historic British cars. This is very much a family attraction, with playgrounds, model cars, rides, a quad bike circuit, a full programme of events and much else besides the more than 300 old and not so old vehicles housed in a large and striking contemporary building.

Motoring heritage at Gaydon

The return to Stratford via minor roads and the B4086 passes through the large village of Wellesbourne, where two final attractions demand attention. The great waterwheel of **Wellesbourne Watermill** can be observed in action powering an array of machinery and producing flour which can be bought. On the far side of the village, an old bunker has been converted into the **Wellesbourne Wartime Museum** (Sunday 10am–4pm), with all kinds of reminders of the time when it was part of Wellesbourne Mountford RAF station.

Route 6

*Grevel's House,
Chipping Campden*

In and out of the Cotswolds

Stratford – Welford-on-Avon – Hidcote Manor Garden
– Chipping Campden – Broadway – Evesham – Pershore (**32 miles/51km**) *See map on pages 44–5*

Welford-on-Avon

To the west of Stratford, the old A439, now downgaded
to a more tranquil B439, parallels the Avon in the direction of Evesham. After 4 miles (6.5km), a minor road to
the left crosses a narrow stone bridge into the long main
street of **Welford-on-Avon**. Welford has expanded in recent times, but still has plenty of black and white thatched
cottages, both along the main road and lining the lane leading to the church. The church is partly Norman, but much
restored in the 19th century. Its 14th-century lychgate, one
of the oldest in the country, has now been replaced by a
replica. The waters of the Avon are controlled by a weir
and a modern lock, while the village's remaining mill
has been turned into a private residence. On the village
green stands a tall maypole, the latest of a long line of may-
poles which have been danced around over the years.

Hidcote delights

The road runs south from Welford past Long Marston,
joining the B4362 just before Mickleton, the first village
in Gloucestershire. At the exit from Mickleton, turn left
up the minor road climbing the steep Cotswold escarpment and follow signs to ★★★ **Hidcote Manor Garden**
(National Trust; April to September daily except Tuesday
and Friday 11am–7pm, October 11am– 6pm; also Tuesday in June and July). Hidcote's reputation as one of the
foremost examples of English garden style ensures it a
constant stream of visitors from all over the world.

Hidcote was the creation of a great horticulturalist and
plant hunter, Lawrence Johnstone, an American who took

British nationality in 1900. He bought the manor house at Hidcote 600ft (180m) up on the exposed plateau of the Cotswolds after serving in the Boer War. In the years leading up to World War I, he set to work creating a whole series of sheltered areas enclosed by hedges of beech, yew and holly which he then filled with an array of carefully chosen plants. His creativity as a plantsman is honoured by the naming of numerous shrubs and flowers which have helped carry Hidcote's fame into the world. A delightful day can easily slip by in exploration of the intricate interconnecting spaces which lie to either side of the great Theatre Lawn. Intimate outdoor 'rooms' contrast with the great avenue of the Long Walk and views out into the idyllic

Hidcote's 'stilt avenue'

countryside beyond the garden boundary. Walls, hedges, circular pools, a gazebo and a 'stilt avenue' of clipped hornbeams give much of the garden a strongly architectural character, in contrast to the controlled wildness of the arboretum or the luxuriant planting which follows the tiny stream meandering across the site.

Hidcote Manor Garden is a hard act to follow, but neighbouring ★★ **Kiftsgate Court** (April, May, August and September, Wednesday, Thursday, Sunday and Bank Holiday Mondays 2–6pm; June and July, Wednesday, Thursday, Saturday and Sunday noon–6pm) succeeds. The late 19th-century Cotswold stone house dominates a garden

Kiftsgate Court and view

laid out from the 1920s onward by Heather Muir, a friend of Lawrence Johnstone and fellow plant enthusiast. Like Hidcote, the garden consists largely of a series of compartments, protected from the winds battering the exposed site on the very edge of the Cotswold escarpment by hedges and tree planting. Unlike Hidcote, laid out on more or less level ground, the garden makes use of the steep slope, and there are magnificent views north and west over the Vale of Evesham. In contrast to Hidcote, the planting is less controlled, more personal, with a great emphasis on colour. The famous Kiftsgate Rose has grown to an extraordinary size, covering about a quarter of an acre (1,000 sq. metres) and reaching a height of 50ft (15m).

Minor roads lead southwest to ★★★ **Chipping Campden**, one of the finest and best preserved medieval towns in the country. In the late Middle Ages, Campden prospered on the wool trade, its most prominent citizen of the time, William Grevel, earning the epithet 'the flower of the wool merchants of all England'. Grevel died in 1401; he is commemorated by a brass in the parish church while **Grevel's House** with its two-storeyed bay window still adorns the beautiful curve of the High Street.

Another famous resident was Sir Baptist Hicks whose great early 17th-century house to the south of the church was destroyed in the Civil War, though the pepperpot pavilions of the gateway still stand. **St James' Church** is one of the finest of all Cotswold wool churches, rebuilt in the 15th century in a wonderfully harmonious Perpendicular style. Close by, raised above road level, is a charming terrace of **almshouses** of 1612.

Almshouses and the church

Relatively remote from big towns and railways, Chipping Campden retained its archaic character into the 20th century, and it was this that attracted adherents of the Arts and Crafts movement to settle here and continue or revive traditional craft skills. It is largely due to the influence of C.R. Ashbee's Guild of Handicrafts, established here in 1902, that the town enjoys such a perfect state of preservation, with few modern intrusions such as jarring shopfronts. The High Street is a continuous experience of minor architectural pleasures, from humble Cotswold cottages to the occasional grand Georgian mansion. The focal point is the **Market Hall**, built by Sir Baptist in 1627; its arches once sheltered traders in cheese, butter and poultry. The **Silk Mill** occupied by Ashbee and his followers is now a silver workshop and also has a small museum devoted to the doings of the Guild.

The Market Hall

High above the town to the northwest is **Dover's Hill**, the site of the rough and rustic games initiated by a local eccentric, Robert Dover, in 1612. Known as the Cotswold Olympicks, they were suppressed in strait-laced Victorian times, but revived in 1951. They take place on the last weekend in May or the first in June, and after the shin-kicking and greasy pole climbing is over there is a grand procession and much merry-making in the town far below.

The B4081 leads from Chipping Campden up to the main A44 from Stow-on-the-Wold to Evesham, which should be followed to the turning for ★ **Broadway Tower Country Park** (April to October 10am–6pm). Laid out along the top of the escarpment, the park has animal enclosures and other attractions and offers a fabulous panorama across the broad Vale of Evesham to the faraway Malvern Hills, and, on a clear day, to even more distant heights: Clee Hill; the Wrekin; the Black Mountains… The views are best studied from the top of the strange structure built for that purpose, Broadway Tower itself. Erected in 1800 for the Earl of Coventry, this splendid turreted folly also has displays on the history of Cotswold sheep and their wool and on William Morris.

Broadway Tower view

The A44 now drops steeply down the escarpment in a series of curves. This is Fish Hill, the scene of many a boiling radiator in the early days of motoring. As the slope becomes gentler at the foot of the hill, the road becomes the 'broad way' which has given its name to one of the most popular of the Cotswold villages. ★★ **Broadway** is actually in Worcestershire, but with all the Cotswold char-

acteristics of mellow stone walls and roof tiles is quite uncharacteristic of that county. Everything here is immaculate, from sensitively designed shop-fronts to tasteful paving and carefully trimmed grass verges. Buildings range from the humblest of cottages to the magnificent Lygon Arms hotel with its great mullioned and transomed windows and cosy interior. Even though there's only a faint echo of the rough and ready rural Cotswolds of yesteryear among the sleek boutiques and antique shops, art galleries and tea rooms, it's still well worth while walking the length of this showpiece village from the green to the thatched cottages at the foot of Fish Hill.

The A44 runs northwestwards away from the Cotswolds through the village of Wickhamford into the very different countryside of the Vale of Evesham with its orchards and market-gardens. ★ **Evesham** itself has expanded to fill the space between the Avon and the bypass which has relieved the town centre of at least some of its traffic. The river swings in a great bend around the town, enclosing it on three sides. An important river crossing from earliest times, Evesham was also the site of one of the most important abbeys in the Midlands, founded in AD714 by Bishop Egwin of Worcester, and much rebuilt over the following centuries. As late as the early 16th century, not long before Henry VIII's Dissolution of all such places, Abbot Clement Lichfield was using the abbey's great wealth to build the great Perpendicular **Bell Tower** which is still the town's most important landmark.

Towards the Avon the land drops gently to the riverside, turned into attractive parkland a century and a half ago and very popular in summertime with boat-people, onlookers and picnickers. Towards the town centre, two churches, All Saints and St Lawrence's, stand in close proximity,

Evesham: Bell Tower and river

one serving the parish, the other the cemetery. A Norman gateway leads into the town centre, where there are a number of good buildings in the broad High Street and elsewhere. The half-timbered Booth Hall is also known as the **Round House**, not because of its shape (definitely rectangular) but because it can be walked right round.

The local **museum** (Monday to Saturday 10am–5pm, Sunday 2–5pm), housed behind the churches in an attractive stone and timber-framed building known as the **Almonry**, has displays on the history of the town and on the Battle of Evesham of 1265, the climatic event which ended the rebellion of Simon de Montfort against Henry III and Prince Edward. De Montfort's forces were trapped in the peninsula formed by the great bend in the Avon and were cut to pieces by the Prince's followers, double their number, as they tried to break out.

Kitchen wares in the Almonry Museum

The mutilated remains of de Montfort were buried in the abbey church, but such was the veneration shown them by populace and pilgrims that they were secretly reburied elsewhere. Shakespeare commented on their power, supposing them to be

chosen from above,
By inspiration of celestial grace
To work exceeding miracles on earth. (Henry VI)

51

To the southwest of Evesham the flat Vale country is dominated by the great flat-topped mound of **Bredon Hill**, immortalised in A.E. Housman's poem *Summertime on Bredon*. The attractive villages crouched at more or less regular intervals around the hill are all worth visiting, none more so than little **Elmley Castle** about 5 miles (8km) from Evesham via the A44 and a minor road. The Norman castle has long since disappeared, but Elmley has an enchanting main street which is more like a square, bordered by charming cottages and by a tree-lined stream.

Lanes lead northwest to ★ **Pershore**, which, like Evesham, is a market centre for the produce of the fertile countryside all around. The accumulated wisdom of the area is passed on a well-reputed College of Horticulture, below which the A44 crosses the Avon and straightaway, without any interruption of suburbs, enters the main street of the little town. Georgian facades abound, a reflection of the town's 18th-century wealth, then largely based on wool. Behind the house-fronts, though, lurks many a more venerable structure, since Pershore, again like Evesham, was an abbey town. In Pershore's case, somewhat more of the **abbey church** survived, though the townspeople seem not to have had the funds to buy or maintain the nave. The remaining combination of tower and chancel looks a little unbalanced, but this is still a fine building, with superb vaulting and some fine bosses.

Pershore: Georgian doorway and Abbey

Route 7

Industrial and cultural metropolis – Birmingham

From the underground platforms of New Street, Britain's busiest mainline station, one set of escalators brings travellers up to concourse level, while another lifts them to the bustling covered shopping centre of the Pallasades. From here, a broad ramp deposits the multi-cultural throng into the very heart of the city at the junction of New Street and Corporation Street, where a continual stream of buses whisks passengers off to all parts of the conurbation.

Victoria Square and the Council House

It's a sudden and stimulating introduction to England's second city, capital of the Midlands. Never glamorous or particularly refined, the city has constantly tried to stay in the forefront of progress, and is still one of the country's major manufacturing centres. Its inventive industrial history is studded with great names like those of James Watt (the steam engine) and Matthew Boulton (gas lighting). In the late 19th and early 20th centuries it prided itself on its civic enterprise; its mayor, Joseph Chamberlain, pushed forward great public works and slum clearance projects, while George Cadbury, the chocolate manufacturer, laid out the model village of Bournville around his factory. Postwar redevelopment failed to beautify the city but has helped keep it commercially vibrant. Birmingham continues to reinvent itself, looking for a new niche as a European city of business and culture.

St Philip's Cathedral with stained glass by Burne-Jones

From New Street, Cannon Street climbs to ★ **St Philip's Cathedral ❶**. Built in 1715, the cathedral is an outstanding example of the English Baroque style with a superb concave-sided tower; its glory is the set of stained glass windows designed by Burne-Jones. Forming a boundary to the pleasant churchyard, **Colmore Row** runs in a straight line between Victoria Square and Snow Hill Station and, more than any other major street in the city centre, has retained much of its dignified late 19th-century character. A short walk beyond Snow Hill Station is the city's Roman Catholic Cathedral, **St Chad's ❷**. The work of England's leading medievalist architect, Augustus Pugin, the twin-towered building is a striking statement in red brick and was the first Catholic cathedral to be built in Britain since the Reformation.

In the other direction, ★★ **Victoria Square ❸** has benefited enormously from its 1993 remodelling. Always the epicentre of the city, it is now a superb stepped pedestrian esplanade, a fitting setting for the great Roman temple of the **Town Hall** (begun in 1832) and the grandiose **Council House** (1879) with its mosaic and its pediment relief entitled *Britannia Rewarding the Manufacturers*

52

of Birmingham. In contrast to these examples of Victorian pomp are the **contemporary sculptures** by Dhruva Mistry. A monumental female figure in bronze, *The River*, sits in the centre of a great pool above a waterfall, flanked by a pair of quizzical sphinxes, the *Victoria Square Guardians*. An equally monumental but even more unfathomable sculpture is Antony Gormley's rusty *Iron Man*.

The paved area leads to **Chamberlain Square**, with the Victorian Gothic Chamberlain Memorial Fountain as its focal point. Other worthies commemorated are James Watt and Joseph Priestley, as well as the local progressive politician Thomas Attwood, his sculpture reclining in apparent comfort on the steps. The dominant buildings here are the great **Central Library** ❹ in brutalist concrete and the ★★ **Museum and Art Gallery** ❺ (Monday to Saturday 10am–5pm, Sunday 12.30–5pm). This is famous above all for its matchless collection of Pre-Raphaelite paintings, with familiar classics like *The Last of England* by Ford Madox Brown and Augustus Egg's *The Travelling Companions*. But there are many other pictures besides, as well as tapestries, jewellery, ceramics, stained glass, fashion, a magnificent coin collection and a terrifying Tyrannosaurus Rex. Visitors can relax in the wonderful **Edwardian Tea Room**.

On the far side of the great atrium of the Library, a broad bridge crosses a section of the city's Queensway to the little octagonal temple of the **Hall of Memory**, within which are the rolls of honour commemorating Birmingham's war dead. Beyond the memorial is the city's newest civic space,

Victoria Square guardian

Inside the Museum

53

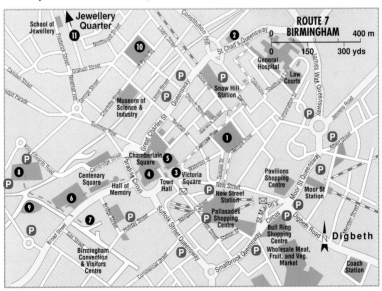

Forward!

Gas Street Basin

National Sea Life Centre

Centenary Square, a setting for the Repertory Theatre and the huge new **International Convention Centre** ❻ whose **Symphony Hall** has been acclaimed as one of the world's finest modern auditoriums. The centrepiece of the square is formed by a monumental resin sculpture by the Birmingham-born artist Raymond Mason. Entitled *Forward*, it is a salute to the enterprise and achievement of the city's people, headed by a heroic worker-figure.

The pedestrian route penetrates the Convention Centre to emerge by the waterside. Birmingham is proud of its mileage of canals, greater than that of Venice. Once a busy hub of this important commercial transport network, **Gas Street Basin** ❼ fell into decay as activity declined, but has now been revived to make a fine setting for the Brindleyplace and Water's Edge developments. Here are boutiques and bars, cafés and restaurants, as well as the 13,000-seat **National Indoor Arena** ❽ and the ★ **National Sea Life Centre** ❾ (from 10am), the latter with the world's first 360° transparent viewing tunnel.

It's possible to walk from the city centre the mile or so northwest into the **Jewellery Quarter**, still the centre of Britain's jewellery industry. On the way is **St Paul's Square** ❿, Birmingham's only surviving Georgian square, dominated by its fine 18th-century church, still with the numbered box pews once occupied by the rich jewellers and other notables of the district. At the far extremity of the Jewellery Quarter, close to the suburban railway station, is the ★ **Discovery Centre** ⓫ (Monday to Friday 10am–4pm, Saturday 11am–5pm). Housed in the former workshops of the family firm of Smith and Pepper, and hardly changed since the beginning of the 20th century, the centre demonstrates in a lively way the skills of the jewellers and their contribution to Birmingham's reputation as the 'workshop of the world'.

Birmingham's environs

In a somewhat unpromising setting between a motorway and Aston Villa's football ground about 2 miles (3km) north of the city centre, red brick ★★ **Aston Hall** (Easter to October daily 2–5pm) is one of the finest Jacobean houses in the Midlands, with a highly picturesque outline of towers and gables. Built for the Royalist Sir Thomas Holte between 1618 and 1631, it was besieged by the Parliamentarians in the Civil War and shot marks can still be seen in its staircase balustrade. There's a splendid Long Gallery, superb plaster ceilings, and much fine furniture.

Aston Hall

Homage is paid to the city's industrial pioneers at ★ **Soho House** (Tuesday to Saturday 10am–5pm, Sunday noon–5pm) about a mile to the northwest of the Jewellery Quarter. Overlooking the site of his manufactory, this was the home of Matthew Boulton, who equipped his Georgian mansion with unheard-of luxuries like flushing toilets and central heating.

Matthew Boulton at Soho House

Many visitors to the Midlands are heading for the vast **National Exhibition Centre** (NEC), close to the International Airport 7 miles (11km) to the east of the city centre. Nearby, what must surely be the biggest collection of British motorbikes in the world is lined up in the ★ **National Motorcycle Museum** (daily 10am–6pm).

To the south of the city centre, in the residential district of Edgbaston, is the ★ **Birmingham Botanical Gardens** (9am–7pm or sunset, from 10am Sunday), designed by the great horticultural writer John Claudius Loudon and opened in 1832. As well as fascinating glasshouses, there are 15 acres (6 hectares) of ornamental gardens, indoor and outdoor aviaries, a playground and an art gallery.

Beyond is the red-brick **University of Birmingham**, dominated by the soaring Italianate Chamberlain Tower, 328ft (100m) high. In the ★★ **Barber Institute** (Monday to Saturday 10am–5pm, Sunday 2–5pm), the university has one of the UK's best private art collections, with pictures ranging from the Italian Renaissance to Gainsborough, Turner, and the French Impressionists.

Further south still is the garden village of **Bournville**, laid out by the Cadburys in the late 19th and early 20th centuries after moving their cocoa factory from its cramped site in the inner city. Their development of rustic looking cottage homes in a leafy setting for their workforce became a model for other projects of this kind at home and abroad and town planners still come here to study their pioneering efforts. Most visitors in Bournville are hungrier for chocolate than history, a demand which ★ **Cadbury World** (tel: 0121 451 4180 for opening hours) does its best to satisfy, though along with tastings and 'free' handouts of chocolate comes the story of chocolate and cocoa and an insight into production methods.

One of many attractions at Cadbury World

Route 8

Coventry

*Coventry Cathedral
and Lady Godiva*

Coventry's fame was established in the Middle Ages, when it was an important trading centre, its prosperity based on wool, and ranking fourth in size among English cities. Today it is known for its industries, for the rebuilding after wartime destruction which produced a great modern cathedral, and, of course, for the tale of Lady Godiva.

Godiva was the wife of a powerful Saxon earl, Leofric. In 1043 the couple founded a Benedictine abbey, but they are better known for the dispute which provoked Godiva into riding naked through the streets, her modesty just about preserved by her long hair and the tact of the citizenry who stayed indoors behind shuttered windows. The exception was a tailor whose curiosity overcame him and whose name has passed into the English language – Peeping Tom. A statue of Godiva graces Coventry's central square, Broadgate, while Tom is commemorated by the clock in the new Cathedral Lanes shopping centre.

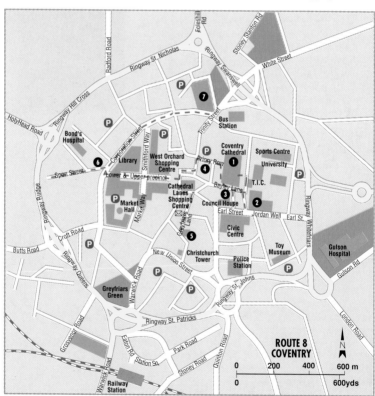

ROUTE 8
COVENTRY

Most visitors come to the city to admire the new ★★★ **Cathedral ❶** (Easter to late September 9.30am–6pm, winter 9.30am–5pm except during services). Close by is the modern **Tourist Information Centre** which is built over one of Coventry's many medieval cellars, and also the **University**, formerly Lanchester Polytechnic.

Coventry Cathedral: the Baptistery window

57

Designed by Sir Basil Spence and built between 1955 and 1962, the cathedral is the successor to the building destroyed in the German air raid of 14 November 1940 in the course of which the old city centre was laid waste. The original intention was to rebuild on the site of the medieval cathedral, but in the event the roofless walls and the 300ft (90m) spire which had survived the raid were kept, linked to the new building by a lofty canopy.

The ★★★ **ruins** of the old cathedral make a poignant introduction to the city. When intact, the building, which became a cathedral only in 1918, was one of the largest parish churches in England. It is now a place of contemplation, a venue for the Mystery Plays performed every two years, and a symbol of the peace and reconciliation.

Old Cathedral ruins

St Michael triumphing over the Devil

Dedicated, like its predecessor, to St Michael, Sir Basil's great new building stands at right angles to the old cathedral and consequently its altar, unconventionally, is at the northern end. It is a structure of immense presence, though its architecture and the artworks which fill it have attracted controversy as well as approval. The walls, like those of the old cathedral and many city buildings, are of the local red sandstone, and the tall main windows are arranged in echelon to allow south light to illuminate the nave. The broad steps leading up to the entrance from the university side are guarded by a striking figure in bronze by Epstein of **St Michael triumphing over the Devil**, while the vast glazed screen is engraved with saints and angels. Inside, the eye is led past the slender columns

Stained glass in the nave

supporting the roof to Graham Sutherland's vast and celebrated tapestry showing a calm Christ in Glory surrounded by the tormented symbols of the Evangelists. The Baptistery has a window of equally awesome scale, with abstract stained glass by John Piper and Patrick Reyntiens and a font consisting of a rugged boulder brought all the way from Bethlehem. Opposite is the star-shaped Chapel of Unity with a marble floor from Sweden. Other chapels include the circular Guild Chapel with a suspended Cross and a view through clear glass of the world beyond, and, in total constrast, the small and inward-looking Chapel of Gethsemane, protected by a screen in the form of the Crown of Thorns which was designed by Spence himself.

The Cathedral and its wealth of artworks speak for themselves, but for a fuller understanding of the building's history and importance there is a fascinating **Visitors Centre**. As well as a spectacular audio-visual show, there are treasures from the old cathedral and gifts from all around the world which recall the international impact and meaning of Coventry's destruction and rebirth.

58

To the south of the Cathedral and opposite the Tourist Information Centre is the **Drapers' Hall**, a 19th-century building which is the successor to much earlier structures which were the headquarters of one of the city's powerful guilds. Beyond is the ★ **Herbert Art Gallery and Museum ❷** (Monday to Saturday 10am–5.30pm, Sunday 2–5pm), more or less contemporary with the Cathedral. Here the main attraction is the Godiva City Exhibition, a lively presentation of the city's history from early days to the present. The fascination which the Godiva story has exercised can be seen in a number of paintings in the first floor gallery, particularly in the glamorous study by the Victorian artist John Collier.

Earl Street rises gently towards the city centre, passing the splendidly self-confident neo-Tudor **Council House** of 1917 with its clock tower and statues of Godiva, Leofric, and Justice. Narrow Hay Lane still has something of the feeling of the medieval city, while in Bayley Lane is one of Coventry's most historic buildings, ★★ **St Mary's Guildhall ❸** (tel: 01203 833328 for opening hours). Built in 1342 and subsequently enlarged as the headquarters of a number of medieval guilds, St Mary's is an evocative reminder of how the city flourished on the proceeds of the wool trade. Its outstanding feature is the first-floor Great Hall, with a spectacular Arras tapestry, a fine window with 15th-century stained glass and a superb timber roof reconstructed after wartime damage. Beneath it is the city's largest vaulted undercroft.

Running northward, Cuckoo Lane leads through the pleasantly leafy area adjoining the two cathedrals. Beyond

The Council House

St Mary's Guildhall: the Council Chamber

the replica **Coventry Cross** stands ★ **Holy Trinity** ❹, the city's only complete medieval church. Sometimes mistaken for the cathedral, it is a substantial building, mostly Perpendicular in style though much restored in the 19th century. The spire, one of the three that make the city skyline so distinctive, reaches a height of 237ft (70m).

The lane alongside the church opens into busy **Broadgate** with the statue of Godiva. Just along Greyfriars Lane is another of the city's outstanding late medieval buildings, ★ **Ford's Hospital** ❺ (10am–5pm). This wonderful timber-framed structure with its courtyard and exuberantly decorative carving was founded as an almshouse in 1509 and still carries out this function.

Ford's Hospital

Broadgate occupies part of the site of the much bigger market place of medieval times and is the point at which vehicular traffic meets the extensive pedestrianised areas of the city centre. Prosperous prewar Coventry was already making plans for an ambitious redevelopment of its central area; the German bombs provided the opportunity, and rebuilding began almost as soon as the war ended, with the whole of the city centre enlosed within a partly elevated ring road. A great **pedestrian precinct** in the form of a cross (two arms of which were originally ordinary streets) stretches gently downhill from Broadgate. Nowadays it is nothing unusual, but in the 1950s it was revolutionary and attracted world-wide attention with its layout on two levels, its sophisticated detailing, tree planting, public sculpture, and an upper-level circular café.

Life in the precinct　　**59**

Beyond the Lower Precinct and marking the approach to Spon Street is **St John's Church** ❻; it is said that the expression 'sent to Coventry' originated here, when Civil War Scottish prisoners were housed here and found local people's attitudes distinctly unfriendly. **Spon Street** has a fascinating array of timber-framed buildings, some of which have been moved here from other parts of the city. Nearby **Hill Street** has more interesting old buildings including another almshouse, Bond's Hospital, and early 19th-century workshops.

Spon Street contrasts

The city centre's second major museum can be reached via Corporation Street. The ★★ **Museum of British Road Transport** ❼ (10am–5pm) has hundreds of cars, bicycles, motorbikes and other vehicles and exhibits which evoke Coventry's special contribution to the development of the motor vehicle. In 1896, with Daimler, the city was the birthplace of the British car industry, and in its heyday was the home of famous names like Alvis, Hillman, Humber, Jaguar, Norton, Riley, Rover, Singer, Standard, Triumph and many more. Production continues, although the marques are different. The museum also has a 'Blitz Experience' which brings to life the horrifying events of the night of 14 November 1940.

Stratford and the Cult of Shakespeare

Honoured in his own time, Shakespeare was appreciated in the town of his birth (in 1564) and death (in 1616) to the extent that the famous life-size bust was unveiled in Holy Trinity Church only months after his burial. Six years later the strolling players called The King's Men came to pay homage to their old colleague, though the puritanical town council forbade them to put on any sort of performance, and, grotesquely, went so far as to pay them the sum of six shillings not to do so.

Shakespeare

But Shakespeare's elevation to a cult figure and the promotion of Stratford as a literary shrine and place of pilgrimage had to wait until the 18th century. In 1741 a funerary monument was placed in Westminster Abbey and around the same time visitors started to search out the places in Stratford most closely associated with Shakespeare. Supposedly planted by him, the mulberry tree in the garden of his home of New Place became an object of veneration, with people demanding to see it and breaking off twigs as souvenirs. After the testy owner of the house had spitefully cut down the tree its wood was made into readily marketable souvenirs by an enterprising local man. Part of it was turned into a box in which was placed the Freedom of Stratford given to the greatest Shakespearean actor of his age, David Garrick (1717–79).

61

The Garrick Jubilee

It was Garrick, more than anyone, who made Stratford into Shakespeare's shrine; in September 1769 he organised what were intended to be magnificent Jubilee celebrations, with lavish dinners, processions, pageants, fireworks, a masked ball and a horse race. As so often in England, the weather had its own plans; rain, rain and more rain drenched the fashionable visitors and their fine costumes and filled the Avon until its banks burst, flooding the meadows where a great timber pavilion had been erected to house the glittering programme of events. But Garrick and his guests struggled gamely on, and were rewarded on the final day by the rain abating. The horse race was run and some of the fireworks at last ignited. But, strangely, no-one had thought of putting on a Shakespeare play, though there was plenty of doggerel recited along the lines of:

Taking in the sights

'*Sacred be thy shrine, Avonian Willy, bard divine!*'

Invited to return and make the Jubilee an annual event, Garrick graciously declined.

Housing Shakespeare

The Garrick Jubilee had put Stratford firmly on the map, and in the late 18th century there was a steady stream of visitors. The tenants of Shakespeare's birthplace in Henley

Hamlet

Performance poster

The Royal Shakespeare Theatre

Street were happy to show people round, displaying the weapon with which he allegedly shot a deer in nearby Charlecote Park and the sword he wore when playing Hamlet. For a small consideration, pieces could be sliced of the very chair on which the Bard had sat.

Throughout the 19th century Stratford attended to its greatest son in two ways. Firstly, attempts were made to rectify the great omission of the Garrick Jubilee by staging the plays in an appropriate setting. A 'National Monument and Mausoleum to the immortal memory of Shakespeare' was proposed in 1820, though the week-long Tercentenary celebrations of 1864 still had to take place in a temporary pavilion. This time, as well as balls and balloon ascents, there were performances of the plays. A few years later, Charles Edward Flower, a member of the local brewing dynasty, bought the site by the Avon where Garrick's Rotunda had stood, and by 1879 the Memorial Theatre was ready, its skyline of towers and gables an exotic addition to the Stratford skyline.

Paralleling this belated attention to the plays came care for the buildings associated with Shakespeare. In 1847 the place of his birth was purchased for the nation, and its restoration begun not long after. Other purchases followed, Nash's House and the site of New Place in 1862, Anne Hathaway's Cottage in 1892, Harvard House in 1909. The modern Shakespeare Centre for serious study and research was added to the birthplace in 1964 and the lavish Visitors' Centre in 1981.

Burnt out in 1926, the original Memorial Theatre was replaced in 1932 by the present Royal Shakespeare Theatre, moored like a great Art Deco liner on the banks of the Avon, a once controversial building which has fulfilled its role admirably and become an essential part of the Stratford scene.

Warwickshire in the History of the Nation

Its central location in the kingdom, together with the presence here of powerful and flamboyant personalities, has meant that Warwickshire has played a disproportionately important part in the course of English history, above all at the end of the Middle Ages and in Tudor times. This adds immensely to the fascination of its historic sites, particularly the great castles at Kenilworth and Warwick.

Not long after its use as a royal base during the 1266 siege of de Montfort's forces in Kenilworth, the castle at Warwick passed into the hands of the Beauchamp family. It was the tenth Earl of Warwick, Guy de Beauchamp, whose dark complexion caused him to be dubbed 'the Black Dog of Arden' by one of Edward I's retinue of attractive young men, Piers Gaveston. Beauchamp's revenge was terrible; in 1312 Gaveston was apprehended and tried at the castle, then beheaded at nearby Blacklow Hill.

Thomas Beauchamp, the 11th Earl of Warwick, fought at the great battles of Crecy and Poitiers, while the 12th Earl, Richard Beauchamp, was responsible in 1431 for the trial and execution of Joan of Arc. Richard's tomb is the showpiece of the Beauchamp Chapel in Warwick's St Mary's Church. On the extinction of the Beauchamp male line, the title passed in 1450 to Richard Neville, the eldest son of the Earl of Salisbury, known as 'Warwick the Kingmaker' for his role in the Wars of the Roses.

Tomb of Richard Beauchamp

This *'impudent and shameless Warwick... proud setter up and puller down of kings'* (Shakespeare, Henry VI Part 3) was a strikingly tall and powerfully built figure, a lavish host, a talented soldier and sailor, and above all a master of intrigue. His talents were first deployed in the Yorkist cause, but in 1455 he was forced to flee to Calais when the deposed King Henry VI recovered from a bout of insanity. Returning to England, he was instrumental in defeating the royal army at the Battle of Northampton in 1460 and placing his cousin, the son of the Duke of York, on the throne as Edward IV. Edward's personality was as forceful as that of his older relative, in whose dynastic intrigues he declined to take his allotted part. An attempt to coerce the king by incarcerating him at Warwick failed, and the Kingmaker was forced to flee to France again, where he concluded an alliance with his old enemy, Margaret of Anjou. A second invasion of England now took place. Gathering his forces at his castle just before Easter 1471, Warwick set out southwards to confront King Edward's army, but in spite of numerical superiority he was defeated and slain at the Battle of Barnet. Not long after, Margaret of Anjou's supporting army was utterly routed at the bloody Battle of Tewkesbury, close to where the Avon joins the Severn.

Warwick Castle

The Battle of Barnet

The Buildings of Shakespeare Country

Visitors in search of traditional English building in brick, stone and timber will find it in the villages and towns of Warwickshire and the Vale of Evesham. Beneath its gloriously extravagant thatched roof, Anne Hathaway's Cottage at Shottery, just outside Stratford-upon-Avon, has a timber frame infilled partly with brick and partly with wattle-and-daub. No cottage, but a prosperous farmhouse, it deserves its fame but it is far from being an isolated example; villages all over the vales and low rolling hills of the area can boast buildings of similar quality and attractiveness dating from the 15th century onwards.

Timber framing in Alcester

Most timber-framing is square in pattern, leaving large spaces to be filled and plastered, but more prosperous owners were able to build walls which are half-timbered or studded, with close-spaced uprights and less infill, an obviously more expensive procedure because of the need for far more timber. Many timber buildings have upper floors picturesquely jettied out over the lower floors, and some have carved decoration, though this is rarely as exuberant as in the counties further west. Particularly in towns, and above all in Stratford with its exceptionally rich heritage of such building, the timber-frame was often covered in the 18th century with a coat of plaster or stucco. This disguise was stripped off in Victorian times and later, when timber once again became fashionable. The stark contrast of black timbers and bright white infill is also a Victorian phenomenon and not historically correct; the Arden oak furnishing the timber was traditionally left to weather to its naturally silver colour, while the infill was often painted dull pink or ochre. Careful inspection of a number of timber buildings in and around Stratford will reveal that they stand on a plinth of blueish-grey stone from the once famous quarries at Wilmcote.

Bare brick at the Shakespeare Countryside Museum

Despite the popular black-and-white image, the most frequent building material in Shakespeare country is brick. Baked from the clays which occur almost everywhere, it is consequently varied in colour, though a bright orange predominates. As well as innumerable humble homes, there are fine examples of elaborate early construction in brick in such great houses as Compton Wynyates, Charlecote Park, and Aston Hall.

On the southern fringe of the area, silvery or honey-coloured Cotswold stone is justly famous for its appearance, workability and weathering qualities. It gives a wonderfully harmonious appearance to sophisticated little towns like Chipping Campden and Broadway. Further east are stones of fascinatingly varied colouring, like the ironstones used at Farnborough Hall or in the villages around Edge Hill.

Festivals, Events and Entertainment

Birmingham Repertory Theatre

Theatre

The highlight of many a visit to Shakespeare Country is obviously a performance at Stratford's **Royal Shakespeare Theatre** (Box office tel: 01789 295623). The theatre has three auditoriums: the Royal Shakespeare itself presents superb interpretations of the Shakespeare repertoire, as does the **Swan Theatre**, a galleried space with much of the atmosphere of an Elizabethan theatre; the Swan also has performances of other classics. Finally, **The Other Place** is a modern and intimate setting for a variety of often highly innovative productions. The Stratford season runs from November to late August.

65

Richard III

Birmingham has several venues of more than local importance. The **Birmingham Hippodrome** (tel: 0121 622 7486) is the Midlands home of Welsh National Opera and the Birmingham Royal Ballet, while the modern **Birmingham Repertory Theatre** (tel: 0121 236 4455) claims an international reputation for innovative productions of the highest quality. The **Alexandra Theatre** (tel: 0121 643 3186), a major touring venue, stages a full range of musicals, comedies and drama, often of West End productions, while the **Birmingham Stage Company** (tel: 0121 643 9050) is the professional repertory company based at the city's Old Rep Theatre.

Festivals

In late April, **Stratford** celebrates Shakespeare's birthday in style. Coventry's **Godiva Procession** in early June is partly a re-enactment of the famous ride, partly a street parade, while in mid-June the ruins of the old Cathedral make an inspiring setting for the medieval **Mystery Plays**. Birmingham's summer **Jazz Festival** brings some of the world's greatest performers to the city.

Birmingham blues

Food and Drink

Opposite: at the Dirty Duck in Stratford

There are few regional specialities to be found in Shakespeare Country, but the area's location in the centre of England has meant that it has always been well supplied with fine ingredients from the whole of the country as well as being open to every kind of culinary influence. The Vale of Evesham is, of course, renowned for its superb fruit and market garden produce, though the vast acreage of its famous asparagus has diminished over recent years. Nevertheless it's still worth looking out for Evesham asparagus – thinner than the East Anglian variety – in season (end May and June) in markets and roadside stalls, and many local pubs and restaurants incorporate it into their menus.

There are excellent local beers and the crop from the fruit trees of the Vale of Evesham is turned into cider and its pear equivalent, perry.

The popularity of the area means that there is a good variety of places to eat even in the smaller towns and in some villages. Of the large cities, Birmingham in particular has an astonishing range of ethnic eating places and can boast of being the British capital of Balti cuisine.

Mongolian influence in Birmingham

Balti fare in Leamington

67

Restaurant selection

This is just a small selection of restaurants located in or around some of the towns and villages covered in this guide. They are listed according to the following price categories: £££ = expensive; ££ = moderate; £ = inexpensive.

Birmingham
Chung Ying, 16–18 Wrottesley Street, tel: 0121 622 5669. Old-established Cantonese restaurant in the middle of the city's Chinese quarter with a 300-item menu including such exotic fare as frogs' legs and steamed eel. ££. **Left Bank**, 79 Broad Street, tel: 0121 643 4464. A spacious restaurant with an wide range of sophisticated meals. Close to International Convention Centre. ££. **Maharaja**, 23 Hurst Street, tel: 0121 622 2641. Indian restaurant with a long-standing reputation for fine food from North India. Handy for the Hippodrome. £. **Shimla Pinks**, 214 Broad Street, tel: 0121 633 0366. Indian food served in the cool modern ambience of a converted car showroom. Convenient for the International Convention Centre. £

Broadway
Dormy House, Willersey Hill, tel: 01386 825711. On the wooded slopes of the Cotswold escarpment overlooking Broadway, this luxury country hotel in a 17th-century farmhouse has a restaurant to match. There's an excellent choice of English cooking with a French touch; bar meals also served. £££. **Lygon Arms**, High Street, tel:

01386 852255. This famous hotel in the very centre of this sophisticated Cotswold village has a restaurant of equally high reputation in its Great Hall. Meals are served beneath its barrel vault and minstrels' gallery, and the wine list draws on the resources of the world's vineyards. £££.

Lygon Arms in Broadway

In and around Evesham

Evesham Hotel, Coopers Lane, off Waterside, tel: 01386 765566. This mostly Georgian hotel goes back to Tudor times while the Cedar Restaurant has a Regency feel. A good choice of food and an accompanying wine list of incredible scope. Buffet lunches available. £££. **The Mill**, Anchor Lane, Harvington, 4 miles north of Evesham. This is a hotel as well as an attractive restaurant in what was an 18th-century malting mill, with lawns running down to the Avon. Menu with strong French influence. £££.

Kenilworth

Restaurant Bosquet, 97a Warwick Road, tel: 01926 852463. Consisting of just two rooms in a terraced house, this outstanding French restaurant has built a faithful local clientele with its Gascon-orientated cuisine. Closed Sunday and Monday and most of August. £££. **Simpson's**, 101 Warwick Road, tel: 01926 864567. A welcoming atmosphere and a modern interpretation of classic dishes are among the merits of this attractive restaurant. Closed Saturday lunchtime, Sunday and Bank Holidays. ££.

Leamington Spa

Lansdowne, 87 Clarendon Street, tel: 01926 450505. Traditional food served in the traditional setting of a stucco'ed Regency corner house. The choice is limited but the food excellent. ££. **Les Plantagenets**, 15 Dormer Place, tel: 01926 451792. A French patron presides over this attractive restaurant in the lower ground floor of a Regency house, and classic French dishes are the ones to go for. ££.

Al fresco in Leamington

In and around Stratford-upon-Avon

Billesley Manor, Billesely, off A46, 3 miles west of Stratford, tel: 01789 279955. The Stuart Restaurant of this 16th-century manor house hotel serves reliable food in its large panelled room. £££. **Liason**, 1 Shakespeare Street, tel: 01789 293400. An attractive modern restaurant set in what was once a Methodist chapel and later a motor museum. Sophisticated cooking both à la carte or from a sensibly short fixed-price menu. Bouillabaisse with a chive and champagne sabayon is highly recommended. £££. **The Opposition**, 13 Sheep Street. tel: 01789 269980. This understandably popular bistro has straightforward, tasty food at affordable prices and its prompt service makes it a good bet for theatre-goers. ££.

In and around Warwick
Findons, 7 Old Square, tel: 01926 411755. Home-smoked specialities and fresh fish dishes are a speciality of this restaurant housed in a listed Georgian building in Warwick's town centre. ££. **Mallory Court**, Harbury Lane, Bishop's Tachbrook, 3 miles (5km) southeast, tel: 01926 330214. An early 20th-century neo-Tudor country house hotel with a panelled restaurant serving a superb choice of modern French cuisine. Afternoon tea is served in the 10-acre (4-hectare) gardens. £££.

Pub and café selection
Coventry
Bunty's, 14–16 Hay Lane. Close to the Cathedral, a friendly café with fine cakes which can be consumed at outside tables. Highly recommended.

Bunty's in Coventry

In Stratford
Dirty Duck, Waterside. The classic actors' pub, always full of theatrical hangers-on and extremely popular. **Slug and Lettuce**, 38 Guild Street. Despite its repulsive name this is a highly successful and consequently popular pub, an excellent venue for a pre-theatre meal, though it gets very crowded with the smart young set later on.

69

Other Shakespeare Country pubs
The Castle, Edge Hill. Sanderson Miller's 18th-century mock castle makes a characterful pub, with a drawbridge leading to turreted WCs. There's a play house in the garden and fine views. **Queen Elizabeth**, Elmley Castle. A fine old-fashioned pub in this pretty village at the foot of Bredon Hill. There's a restaurant too which makes good use of local ingredients from the Vale of Evesham. **Butcher Arms**, Farnborough. Good food as well as properly kept beers in this nicely renovated old pub close to Farnborough Hall in southeast Warwickshire. **Howard Arms**, Ilmington. A fine stone-built pub in this most attractive village set in a valley reaching into the Cotswold escarpment. Flagstone floors, timber beams and an inglenook fireplace contribute to the snug atmosphere and there's delicious food as well. **Old Bull**, Inkberrow. The prototype *Archers* pub, a Tudor building with bulging walls and all the appropriate features plus any amount of *Archers* memorabilia. Good simple food and outside tables. **The Navigation**, Lapworth. The pub's lawn goes down to the canalside and the place is popular with both locals and canal cruisers. There are generous helpings of bar food plus barbecues, jazz, Morris dancing and even theatricals on occasion. **Bull's Head**, Wootton Wawen. The Bull's Head has superb but not particularly cheap food as well as a good range of beers.

Queen Elizabeth, Elmley Castle

Bull's Head, Wootton Waven

The Grand Union Canal

Active Pursuits

Canals and rivers

Shakespeare Country's greatest recreational asset is its network of navigable waterways. The Avon was one of the first rivers in the country to be improved; in 1636–9 the section downstream from Stratford was made navigable for 30-ton vessels, enabling local agricultural products to be sent to Bristol and beyond, and exotic imports like sugar and tobacco to be transported inland.

Negotiating Hatton Locks

In 1816, Stratford was reached by a wholly artificial waterway, the Stratford-on-Avon Canal. From its junction with the Worcester & Birmingham Canal at Kings Norton in the Birmingham suburbs this ran 25½ miles (40km) via a connection with the Grand Union Canal at Lapworth to a spacious basin at Stratford, where it joined the Avon navigation. Like many British waterways, both the Avon and the Stratford Canal fell into decay and disuse and were only rescued by strenuous efforts on the part of dedicated individuals. The Avon navigation was fully restored by 1974, exactly 100 years after the last commercial craft reached Stratford, while the canal was reopened by the Queen Mother in 1964. A plaque by the side of the Stratford basin records the contribution made by prisoners from Wormwood Scrubs and Birmingham to its restoration.

As well as linking Shakespeare country to the national waterway network, these re-openings made it possible to take circular trips around the 'Avon Ring', linking Stratford with Tewkesbury, Worcester and Kings Norton. This is a fascinating journey, passing many of the places described in this guide, as well as taking in many locks, several aqueducts, including the one at Edstone, the longest in England. Birmingham is at the hub of the national canal system, with connections to all parts of the country.

There are a number of ways of experiencing Shakespeare Country from the water, passively aboard a sightseeing or dining cruiser, or more actively by hiring a narrowboat for a day or a longer period.

Cruise firms: **The River Centre**, Hampton Mill, Evesham, tel: 0973 838526. Themed cruises and holidays on the Severn as well as the Avon. **Second City Canal Cruises Ltd**, Kingston Row, Birmingham, tel: 0121 236 9811. 'Heritage Cruises' with commentary. **Sherborne Wharf**, Sherborne Street, Birmingham, tel: 0121 455 6163. Party hire and trips. **Stratford Marina Ltd**, The Boatyard, Clopton Bridge, Stratford-upon-Avon, tel: 01789 269669). Daytime or evening cruises.

Getting through Stratford

Hire firms: **Alvechurch Boat Centres Ltd**, Scarfield Wharf, Alvechurch (on the Birmingham and Worcester Canal near Kings Norton), tel: 0121 445 2909; **Anglo Welsh**, Wootten Wawen, tel: 01564 793 427; **Bidford Boats**, Bidford-on-Avon, tel: 01789 773205; **Evesham Marina**, Evesham (tel: 01386 47813); **Kate Boats**, The Boatyard, Nelson Lane, Warwick, tel: 01926 492968.

Cycling

The lanes and minor roads of most of the area make cycling a pleasant experience, with just enough gradients to add stimulation. The Warwickshire Feldon Cycleway explores this part of the countryside and 5 miles (8km) of old railway line between Stratford and Long Marston has been made into the Greenway for cyclists as well as walkers and horse riders.

Cyclists should take care on the towpaths

Walking

Most of the area is covered by a close-knit network of footpaths and bridleways, particularly around Kenilworth and Warwick, and there are endless possibilities for short to medium length walks. Recent years have seen the designation of a number of long-distance trails, most of them waymarked. The Centenary Way, created on the 100th anniversary of Warwickshire County Council, runs 100 miles (160km) across the county from Kingsbury Water Park in the north to Meon Hill in the south, while the Heart of England Way enters the area to the south of Solihull and links with the Cotswold Way at Chipping Campden.

Burton Dassett Country Park

The Cotswold Way itself follows the spectacular Cotswold escarpment all the way from Campden to Bath. The Monarch's Way traces the flight of King Charles I from west to east across Warwickshire after the Battle of Worcester, and the MacMillan Way briefly enters the eastern part of the area on its more than 200-mile (350-km) journey along the outcrop of England's Jurassic rocks from Abbotsbury in Dorset to Oakham in Rutland. Finally, there are canal towpaths and a footpath along the Avon.

Getting There

By car

At the heart of England, Shakespeare Country is almost too accessible by road. The area has long been fringed by motorways, M5 to the west, M1 and M6 to the north and east. More recently, the M42 has orbited Birmingham to the south and the M40 from London and Oxford has penetrated to the centre of the region, with junction 15 giving direct access to Stratford and to Warwick and Leamington. A major road, the A46, of variable quality but bypassing all the towns, runs more or less parallel to the course of the Avon from near Tewkesbury to Coventry linking the M5 and M6. At Evesham, the A46 connects with the A44, a good alternative for those visiting the south of the region from either the Worcester direction or from Oxford. Visitors coming from the south have the option of turning off the A44 at Chipping Norton onto the relatively uncongested A3400, which cuts straight through the heart of the region via Shipston-on-Stour to Stratford.

On the road again

By coach

Most of the towns in the area are linked by daily National Express coach services to major cities in the rest of England, usually with a change at Birmingham's Digbeth coach station. There are several direct services a day from Stratford/Warwick to London Heathrow as well as to London Victoria Coach Station. National Express enquiries tel: 0891 910910

By rail

All the larger towns in the area have a railway station. There are direct services from London Paddington to Evesham, Stratford, Leamington Spa (change here for Warwick); from London Marylebone to Warwick; and from London Euston to Birmingham and Coventry. A residual network of suburban lines with terminuses at Stratford and Redditch links a number of towns and villages to Birmingham New Street or Snow Hill. Bromsgrove is on the Cross-Country line between Bristol and Birmingham. Birmingham New Street has frequent connections to all parts of Britain. For all rail enquiries tel: 0345 484950.

Heading for Stratford

By air

Birmingham International Airport (main terminal tel: 0121 767 7145) has internal UK flights, daily New York and Chicago flights, as well as scheduled and charter connections with more than 40 European cities. The airport has direct access to Birmingham International railway station on the Birmingham–London Euston main line and is close to junction 6 on the M42 motorway.

73

Getting Around

Public transport

It is possible to explore Shakespeare Country by public transport but it will require careful planning, and visitors will find themselves tempted to either bring their own car or hire one unless they are happy to be confined to the main towns, where admittedly many of the attractions are concentrated. There are far fewer services on Sunday than on weekdays.

Local bus services are nearly all run by Stagecoach, with details available from Tourist Information Centres or direct from Stagecoach's Rugby office (tel: 01788 535555). The suburban rail lines linking parts of Warwickshire with Birmingham (*see page 73*) are a useful alternative to taking a car through city traffic, though there are few evening services.

Parking in Henley-in-Arden

Car Hire

Evesham: Brooklyn Ford, Four Pools Retail Park, tel: 01386 442525.
Leamington Spa: Avis,Old Warwick Road, tel: 01926 428484.
Stratford: Hertz Station Road, tel: 01789 298827.
Warwick: UCS Longbridge Garage, Stratford Road, tel: 01926 495188.

Taxis

Evesham: M.D.Taxi, Badsey, Evesham, tel: 01926 882965.
Leamington: Spa Taxi Rank, Hamilton Terrace, Holly Walk, tel: 01926 421092.
Stratford: Bridge Street Taxi Rank, tel: 01789 269999.
Warwick: Warwick Taxi Rank, tel: 01926 499966.

Planning the next move

Maps and plans

Ordnance Survey 1:50,000 Landranger Sheets nos. 139 (Birmingham), 140 (Coventry) 150 (Worcester, The Malverns & Surrounding Area) and 151 (Stratford-upon-Avon & Surrounding Area) cover the whole area described in this guide. All rights of way on footpaths and bridleways are shown and other information of interest to visitors is highlighted.

A special Ordnance Survey Cotswold Tourist Map at a scale of 1 inch to 1 mile covers most of the Cotswolds including the Chipping Campden/Broadway area. A large scale 1:25,000 Explorer Map Sheet 14, Malvern Hills and Bredon Hill, covers the Pershore and Bredon Hill area in great detail.

The free town plans supplied by Tourist Information Centres are adequate for a brief visit.

Facts for the Visitor

Tourist Information

Shakespeare Country is generously provided with Tourist Information Centres. They supply a wealth of information on local attractions and seasonal events. Most operate an accommodation booking service. Those marked * are open only in summer.

Birmingham: BCVB Ticket Shop and Information Office 2 City Arcade, B2 4TX, tel: 0121 643 2514; Visitor Information Centre 130 Colmore Row, B3 3AP, tel: 0121 693 6300; National Exhibition Centre, The Piazza, NEC, B40 1NT, tel: 0121 780 4321. **Broadway***: 1 Cotswold Court, The Green, tel: 01386 852937. **Bromsgrove**: Bromsgrove Museum, 26 Birmingham Road, B61 0DD, tel: 01527 831809. **Chipping Campden**: Town Hall, GL55, tel: 01386 841206. **Coventry**: Bayley Lane, CV1 5RN, tel: 01203 832303. **Evesham**: The Almonry Museum, Abbey Gate, WR11 4BG, tel: 01386 446944. **Kenilworth**: The Library, 11 Smalley Place, CV8 1QG, tel: 01926 52595. **Leamington Spa**: the Jephson Lodge, Jephson Gardens, The Parade, CV32 4AB, tel: 01926 311470. **Pershore**: 19 High Street, WR10 1AA, tel: 01386 554262. **Stratford-upon-Avon**: Bridgefoot, CV37 6GW, tel: 01789 293127. **Warwick**: The Court House, Jury Street CV34 4EW, tel: 01926 492212.

At the Court House in Warwick

Guided tours

Stratford-upon-Avon

Shakespeare's Life in Stratford. Informative and entertaining two-hour walk around Stratford led by a Shakespearean actor and director. Contact: Royal Shakespeare Swan Theatre, tel: 01789 412602.

Guide Friday. Open-top double-decker bus tours of Stratford and outlying Shakespeare sites with guide. Contact: Guide Friday Tours, Civic Hall, 14 Rother Street, tel: 01789 294466.

Warwick

The Warwick Society runs highly informative historic walks around the town starting at the Tourist Information Centre (Easter to September each Sunday at 10.45; also Friday and Saturday evenings in July and August; tel: 01926 491343).

Emergencies

In emergency dial 999 for all services.
Warwickshire Constabulary HQ, tel: 01926 415000.
Stratford Police Station, tel: 01789 414111.
Leamington Spa Police Station, tel: 01926 451111.
West Mercia Constabulary HQ (for Evesham area), tel: 0345 444888.

Guide Friday in Stratford

75

Shakespeare Country for Children

The spectacular audio-visual show of **The World of Shakespeare** at Waterside, Stratford (daily from 9.30am, tel: 01798 268885) may whet children's appetite for more of the Bard, and visits to the various Shakespeare houses are not without interest for older children. The Life and Background exhibition at the **Visitors' Centre** puts Shakespeare in the context of his time and makes him more accessible. Going behind the scenes at the **Royal Shakespeare Theatre** is a fascinating experience for all ages, and there may be the chance to dress up.

Falconry at Wilmcote

But when children tire of Shakespearean Stratford, there are many other things in and around the town to hold their attention. In Theatre Gardens is the **Brass Rubbing Centre**, with a large collection of reproduction brasses ideal for producing one's own rubbing. All materials are supplied. The **Teddy Bear Museum** (daily 9.30am–6pm or 5pm in January and February) seems to attract as many adults as children, as does the **Butterfly Farm** (daily 10am–6pm or dusk in winter), claimed to be the largest of its kind in Europe, with up to 1,000 free-flying butterflies and an Insect City. At the **Shakespeare Countryside Museum** in Wilmcote there are thrilling displays of falconry and other activities. There are falcons too at the **Shire Horse Centre** one mile south of the town centre (daily 10am–5pm, closed Thursday and Friday November to February), along with rare farm breeds and the magnificent nags themselves. Further into the countryside are two similar attractions which do their best to keep children busy and entertained. Along with its shops and craft outlets, **Hatton Country World** (daily 10am–5pm) has a farm park, a guinea pig village and a large indoor play centre. To the north of Henley-in-Arden is **Umberslade Children's Farm** (daily late March to late September 10am–5pm), a working farm whose animals are used to young visitors and quite uninhibited by their presence.

Hatton Country World

At **Warwick Castle**, children of all ages will enjoy the Armoury, Torture Chamber and Dungeon, while the 'Kingmaker' attraction is only really suitable for the over-10s. Before visiting the castle it is certainly worth enquiring about any upcoming special events that may be geared to children – tel: 01926 406600 for information.

A quad bike ride at the **Heritage Motor Centre** at Gaydon is popular among the mechanically inclined, while the **National Sea Life Centre** in Birmingham's Brindleyplace (daily 10am onwards) brings vistors into spectacularly intimate contact with the denizens of the deep. Children will also point out that no visit to the region is complete without a chocolate tasting at Birmingham's renowned **Cadbury World** (check opening times tel: 0121 451 4180).

Accommodation

Shakespeare Country is used to visitors and offers an exceptionally wide range of accommodation, though it is perhaps the country house hotels that make a stay here a particularly distinctive experience. Many offer up-to-date comforts and convenience in a mellow setting that seems wholly at one with the local building and landscape heritage. For those with the means, a stay in such a hotel makes a wonderful introduction to the area. Some of the establishments listed in the restaurant section (*see pages 67–8*) offer accommodation of this type. But there are plenty of other possibilities too, from good town hotels and guest houses, to bed-and-breakfast in private homes, self-catering accommodation, and caravan and camp sites.

Most Tourist Information Centres operate an accommodation booking service for which a small charge may be made. For stays on farms, contact Warwickshire Farm Holidays, Crandon House, Avon Dassett, Leamington Spa CV33 0AA, tel: 0295 770652.

Hotel selection

£ £50–£80 per night double
££ £80–£120 per night double
£££ more than £120 per night double

An option in Chipping Campden

Bromsgrove
Pine Lodge Hotel, Kidderminster Road, Bromsgrove B61 9AB, tel: 01527 576600. Immaculately run large hotel just outside the town on A448 in the Kidderminster direction with pool and spa facilities. ££.

Evesham
Salford Hall, 5 miles (8km) north in Abbot's Salford, tel: 01386 871300. Medium-sized hotel set in a Tudor mansion with gatehouse, walled garden, glazed-in courtyard, and plenty of period features like mullioned windows and heraldic stained glass. ££. **Riverside Hotel**, The Parks, Offenham Road, Evesham WR11 5JP, tel: 01386 446200. Welcoming private hotel with attractive decor and standing in 3-acre grounds on the banks of the Avon. Gourmet restaurant with daily change of menu. ££

Leamington Spa
Regent Hotel, 77 The Parade, Leamington Spa, tel: 01926 427231. In the very centre of Leamington, The Regent was the biggest hotel in the world when it was opened in 1819 and owes its name to the gracious dispensation of the Prince Regent. It has played a central part in the spa town's life ever since, undergoing periodic modernisation. Vaults Restaurant in the hotel cellars. ££.

North Cotswolds

Broadway Hotel, The Green, Broadway, tel: 01386 852401. Cosy and welcoming small hotel dating from the late 16th century though its origins go back even further to a medieval monastic establishment. Centrally situated in one of the Cotswolds' most charming and popular villages. ££. **Collin House**, Collin Lane, Broadway, tel: 01386 858354. Tiny, cottagey private hotel just outside Broadway. Some rooms have four-poster beds. ££. **Cotswold House**, The Square, Chipping Campden, tel: 01386 840330. In the main street of this most exquisite of Cotswold towns is this mostly early 19th century hotel, with its tasteful decor featuring many antiques. Dinner in the elegant Garden Room Restaurant may be accompanied by a pianist. ££. **Noel Arms**, High Street, Chipping Campden, tel: 01386 840317. Ancient inn where Charles II sojurned following his defeat at the Battle of Worcester. Mixture of old rooms with antique furniture and modern rooms in rear extension. ££. **Three Ways House**, Mickleton, near Chipping Campden, tel: 10386 438429. Private stone-built hotel in a small Cotswold village. ££.

The Noel Arms

78

In and around Stratford-upon-Avon

Alveston Manor, Clopton Bridge, Stratford-upon-Avon, tel: 01789 204581. This large half-timbered hotel is a landmark on the far bank of the Avon from the Royal Shakespeare Theatre. Part of it dates from the 16th century and it is traditionally held to be the site of the first performance of *A Midsummer Night's Dream*. £££. **Charlecote Pheasant**, Charlecote, Warwick, tel: 01789 470222. Close to Charlecote Park with its herds of deer and Shakespearean associations is this luxury country hotel with accommodation in fine old farm buildings as well as in purpose-built contemporary blocks. Swimming pool. £££. **Shakespeare Hotel**, Chapel Street, Stratford-upon-Avon, tel: 01789 294771. One of the finest buildings in the historic centre of Stratford, the half-timbered Shakespeare dates from the 17th century and could hardly be more atmospheric, though the recently refurbished bedrooms are far from lacking in contemporary comforts. A Forte Heritage hotel. £££. **Stratford House**, 18 Sheep Street, Stratford-upon-Avon CV37 6EF, tel: 01789 268288. This small private hotel in a delightfully furnished Georgian house is conveniently located close to the Avon and the Royal Shakespeare Theatre. ££. **Welcombe Hotel**, Warwick Road, Stratford-upon-Avon, tel: 01789 295252. This grandiose 19th-century Jacobean-style mansion is set in its own spacious parkland just outside Stratford in the direction of Warwick and has many amenities including its own golf course and gourmet restaurant named after a former owner, the historian Sir George Trevelyan. £££.

The Shakespeare Hotel

White Swan, Rother Street, Stratford-upon-Avon, tel: 10789 297022. A key example of Stratford's heritage of half-timbered buildings, the Swan dates from the 16th century and features a wall-painting of that era in its bar. Rooms are mostly in later extensions. ££.

The White Swan

Warwick
The Old Fourpenny Shop Hotel, 27–29 Crompton Street, Warwick, tel: 01926 491360. Highly commended small private hotel in tranquil location. Restaurant and bar with excellent range of beers. £.

Bed and Breakfast selection
North Cotswolds
Whiteacres, Station Road, Broadway, tel: 01386 852320. Hundred-year old house on the edge of Broadway with six bedrooms, some with four-poster beds. Sparlings, Leysbourne, Chipping Campden, tel: 01386 840505. 17th-century house at the end of Chipping Campden's main street with many original features like flagstone floors and old beams. Two bedrooms. Holly House, Ebrington, near Chipping Campden, tel: 01386 593213. Two guest rooms with own entrance in a converted wheelwright's shop in this small village two miles east of Chipping Campden.

79

In and around Stratford
Brook Lodge, 192 Alcester Road, Stratford-upon-Avon, tel: 01789 295988. Close to Anne Hathaway's Cottage and to open country is this immaculately run little guesthouse with 7 rooms. Loxley Farm, Loxley, near Warwick, tel: 01789 840265. Four miles east of Stratford, this is a characterful cruck-framed farmhouse with two guest rooms in a converted barn. Sandbarn Farm, Hampton Lucy, near Stratford-upon-Avon, tel: 01789 842280. In open countryside 4½ miles (7km) northeast of Stratford, this splendid red-brick building with its six guest rooms dates from the 16th century.

B&B in Chipping Campden

In and around Warwick
Forth House, 44 High Street, Warwick, tel: 01926 401512. The two guest rooms of this fine Georgian building in the middle of Warwick are at the rear and consequently tranquil. Pageant Lodge, 2 Castle Lane, Warwick, tel: 01926 491244. Between Warwick's Doll Museum and the Castle entrance, this three-room establishment could not be more central. Dates in part from the 15th century. Fulbrook Edge, Sherbourne Hill, near Warwick, tel: 01926 624242. To the south of the town and close to junction 15 of the M40, this is a country dwelling with a 2½-acre garden and views of the Avon and Cotswolds. Three prettily furnished and spacious rooms.

Index

Accommodation......77–9
Alcester.......................38
Almonry Museum.........5
architecture.................64
Arden..................7, 34–7
Aston Cantlow 35
Atherstone-on-Stour....42
Avon River14, 22, 47, 70
Avoncroft Museum
  of Buildings..............41

Baddesley Clinton
  Hall......................6, 36
Barnet,
  battle of.........11, 30, 63
Birmingham...........52–5
  Aston Hall...............55
  Barber Institute.......55~
  Botanical Gardens....55
  Bournville.................55
  Cadbury World.........55
  Centenary Square .53–4
  Central Library 53
  Chamberlain
    Square 53
  Council House 52
  Discovery Centre......54
  Gas Street Basin 54
  International
    Convention Centre .54
  Jewellery Quarter 54
  Museum and
    Art Gallery.............53
  National Exhibition
    Centre....................55
  National
    Indoor Arena..........54
  National Motorcycle
    Museum 55
  National
    Sea Life Centre 54
  St Chad''s.................52
  St Paul's Square 54
  St Philip's
    Cathedral................52
  Soho House 55
  Town Hall.................52
  Victoria Square.........52
boating....................70–1
Bredon Hill..................51
Broadway................49–50
Broadway Tower
  Country Park 49
Bromsgrove..................41
Burton Dasset
  Country Park 46

Canals.....................70–1
Charlecote Park.......7, 37
children's activities 76

Chipping Campden .48–9
Civil
  War...6, 11, 32–3, 44–5
Clifford Chambers 42
Compton Wynyates.....43
Coventry............9, 56–9
  Bond's Hospital........59
  Cathedral 57–8
  Council House 58
  Drapers Hall 58
  Ford's Hospital.........59
  Herbert Art Gallery and
    Museum 59
  Holy Trinity Church .59
  Museum of British
    Road Transport 59
  St John's Church 59
  St Mary's Guildhall...58
  Spon Street 59
Coughton
  Court.............11, 39–40
cycling.......................71

Dover's Hill 49
Dudley, Robert 11, 25, 33

Earls of Warwick...27, 63
Edge Hill 44
Edge Hill, battle of...44–5
Elmley Castle 51
Evesham...................50–1
Evesham,
  battle of.........8, 11, 51
Evesham,
  Vale of 8, 50, 67

Falconing....................76
Farnborough Hall........46
Feckenham 40
Feldon 7, 27
Foss Way..........10, 14, 42

Gardens....................6–7
Garrick, David.11, 18, 61
Gaydon.......................46
guided tours.................75
Gunpowder Plot 11, 40

Hampton Lucy............36
Hanbury Hall.........7, 41
Hathaway, Anne...........23
Hatton Country
  World.......................36
Hatton Locks...............36
Henley-in-Arden 35
Heritage Motor
  Centre 46
Hidcote
  Manor Garden ..7, 47–8
history 10–11

Honington 42
Honington Hall............43

Inkberrow....................40

Kenilworth
  Castle...6, 11, 32–3, 63
  Kiftsgate Court...........48
Kinwarton 39

Lady Godiva....10, 56, 58
  landscape................5–6, 8
Leamington Spa 31–2
Lucy, Sir Thomas.......37

Mary Arden's
  House...................34–5
Mickleton 47

Neville,
  Richard 6, 11, 30, 63

Packwood House 6, 35–6
Pershore......................51
Preston-on-Stour 42
pubs............................69

Queen
  Ethelfleda 10, 24, 28

Ragley Hall 39
restaurants 67–8

Shakespeare,
  John 15–16, 34–5, 61
Shakespeare,William.......
  ...14–23, 37, 51, 61–2
Shakespeare Countryside
  Museum 34
Shipston-on-Stour 42
Simon de
  Montfort ...8, 11, 51, 33
Snitterfield...................36
Stratford-upon-
  Avon 8, 14–23
Almshouses 21
American
  Fountain 17–18
Anne Hathaway's
  Cottage.............23, 62
Bancroft Gardens........15
Brass Rubbing
  Centre....................22
Clopton Bridge 15
Falcon Hotel 19
Garrick Inn 18–19
Gower Memorial 15
Guild Chapel 21
Hall's Croft...........21–2
Harvard House....18, 62

Holy Trinity
  Church 22, 61
Nash's
  House 19–20, 62
nine-arched bridge....15
Old Bank 19
Royal Shakespeare
  Theatre ..22–3, 62, 65
Shakespeare Centre ..16
Shakespeare Hotel 19
Shakespeare's
  Birthplace...15, 17, 62
Shakespeare's grave .22
Site of
  New Place 20–1, 62
Swan Theatre......23, 65
Town Hall..................19
Visitors' Centre ..16–17
White Swan Hotel 18

Theatre........................65
timber-framing 64
tourist information 75
transport 73–4

Upton House
  and Gardens.........43–4

Walking......................71
Warmington.................46
Wars of the Roses .11, 63
Warwick................24–30
  Beauchamp Chapel...27
  Castle...........6, 28–3, 63
  Castle Bridge 28
  Court House.............25
  Doll Museum............28
  East Gate 27
  Landor House 27
  Lord Leycester's
    Hospital..............25–6
  Market Place 26–7
  Mill Street................28
  Mill Garden 28
  Northgate Street........27
  St John's 28
  St Mary's Church 27
  St Nicholas'
    Church 28
  Warwickshire
    Museum 26–7
  West Gate 25
Warwick the Kingmaker
  see Neville, Richard
Welford-on-Avon........47
Wellesbourne 46
Wimpstone 42
Wootton Waven 35
Worcester and
  Birmingham Canal ...41